Media Trolls, Technology Shamans and Diabolical

Political, Economic and Military Demons

John Stanton

ISBN-10: 1508866358
ISBN-13: 978-1508866367

DEDICATION

Damien and Scylla

INTRODUCTION

Within these pages is a collections of essays written over the course of 2014. They were carried by a number of online publications: Cryptome, Pravda, the Sri Lanka Guardian, Dissident Voice, Scoop, CounterPunch, Intrepid Report and Windows to Russia. Obviously these publications are not mainstream media nor in the lofty class of new media like the Intercept or Buzzfeed. And that's just fine as the audience-base for these websites is not only niche-American locales, but other geographic locations like Asia, Canada and South America. The pieces that appear in the CounterPunches of the world are generally written by all "submitters" for no compensation; that is, they take time out of their "pay days" to write about matters that make them toss and turn at night.

Those sleepless nights revolve around trying to convince those who will read/listen that the powerful--taking form, as say, technologists, pundits and political leaders--are clearly leading humanity on a long doomsday path. The evidence is visible: In the USA and Europe by the not so subtle global covet/overt operations to overthrow "elected" governments like Ukraine and Egypt, with the long view to usher in regime change in Russia and China. The return to expanding nuclear weapons capability in the USA and Russia. The implementation of crushing Austerity programs even as, in the USA, infrastructure degrades. But maybe the negativity I and others express is equally misguided as humanity is now on the cusp of re-engineering itself through genetics and bio-engineering. The properly redesigned human could likely survive well in a world of scarcity, one ravaged by climate change and war. But what would the next-generation humans do with older models like us?

The title of this book refers to Trolls, Shamans and Demons. We listen uncritically to them all at our own collective peril. If we don't listen we hideout in our favorite TV show, video game, chat room or fasten the head phones on to drown them out. We choose to hide from them and now each other. What's to come?

The Temptation of Saint Anthony by Martin Schongauer 1480-1490. Engraving. The Metropolitan Museum of Art, New York.

Public Domain. Retrieved from:

http://commons.wikimedia.org/wiki/File:Schongauer_Anthony.jpg

TABLE OF CONTENTS

Culling the Human Herd in the 21st Century

"There is a de facto redefinition of "the economy" when sharp contractions are gradually lost to standard measures. The unemployed who lose everything…easily fall off the edge of what is defined as "the economy" and counted as such. So do small shop and factory owners who lose everything and commit suicide. And so do the growing number of well-educated students and professionals who leave…all together. These trends redefine the space of the economy. They make it smaller and expel a good share of the unemployed and poor from standard measures. Such a redefinition makes "the economy" presentable, so to speak, allowing it to show a slight growth of GDP per capita.

The reality at the ground level is more akin to a kind of economic version of ethnic cleansing in which elements considered troublesome are dealt with by simply eliminating them. This shrinking and redefinition of economic space so that economies can be represented as being "back on track" holds for a growing number of economies in the European Union and elsewhere [like the United States]… One indication of a people's economic despair is a sharp rise in suicide. This trend is evident in several countries worldwide from India to the United States…

The channels for expulsion vary greatly. They include austerity policies that have helped shrink the economies of Greece and Spain, environmental policies that overlook toxic emissions from enormous mining operations in Norilsk, Russia and the American state of Montana…if our concern is environmental destruction rather that interstate politics, the fact that both these mining operations are heavy polluters matters more than the fact that one is in Russia and the other in the United States…The diverse processes and conditions I include under the notion of expulsion all share one aspect: they are acute. While the abjectly poor worldwide are the most extreme instance, I do include such diverse conditions as the impoverishment of the middle classes in rich countries, the evictions of millions of small farmers in poor countries…Then there are the countless displaced people warehoused in formal and informal refugee camps, the minoritized groups in rich countries who are warehoused in prisons and the able bodied unemployed men and women warehoused in ghettoes and slums…Some are new types of expulsions, such as the 9 million households in the United Stateswhose homes were foreclosed…"

Saskia Sassen's book *Expulsions: Brutality and Complexity in the Global Economy* (Harvard-Belknap Press, May 2014) begins its sobering journey with an Introduction titled, *"The Savage Sorting." The Savage Sorting* seems destined to become the short-form description of 21st Century to be remembered, if at all, in some distant future by a genetically reengineered humanity (and biosphere).

Most television watchers are familiar with programming on National Geographic or Animal Planet that depicts "life in the wild" for non-human animals. Typical scenes from "nature" programming include lions and hyenas hunting down young, old and infirm wildebeests or zebras. Ultimately successful, they engage in a feeding frenzy. Sometimes the prey is still alive as it is being disemboweled by the predators. Chimpanzees attack, kill and eat rivals whilst emitting screams that unsettle the viewer's nerves. Aging grizzly bears are observed losing their prized hunting spots to the young and are left to feed on scraps, themselves destined to be prey for creatures large and small. As the "nature" show goes on, the soothing voice of the human narrator assures the audience that it is all part of the "natural order of things."

That "natural order of things" also includes human-on-human expulsion and extermination. But before touching a bit on the 21st Century culling of the human herd, it is worth noting that human-on-non-human carnage continues into this "modern" century. One of the practices of this new age of enlightenment is "Canned Hunting" in South Africa. European, North Americans and Chinese big game hunters, according to the Guardian newspaper, sometimes sit on the back of pickup trucks and wait for lions— bred for a "guaranteed kill"–to run by or walk up to the truck. In the Guardian's "The lions bred for slaughter: Canned hunting is a fast-growing business in South Africa, where thousands of lions are being bred on farms to be shot by wealthy foreign trophy-hunters," the reader is confronted with a repulsive picture of a happy hunter gloating over a dead lion.

Humans Don't Discriminate, They Eliminate Non-Humans and Humans Equally

Then there is the case of the Gray Wolf in the United States. According to The Wolf that Changed America, "Wolves have been feared, hated, and persecuted for hundreds of years in North America. Before the arrival of Europeans, Native Americans incorporated wolves into their legends and rituals, portraying them as ferocious warriors in some traditions and thieving spirits in others. European Americans, however, simply despised wolves. Many, including celebrated painter and naturalist John James Audubon, believed wolves ought to be eradicated for the threat they posed to valuable livestock. This attitude enabled a centuries-long extermination campaign that nearly wiped out the gray wolf in the continental United States by 1950."

Now that Grey Wolf populations are increasing—thanks to the work of some bright humans–denizens in American states like Idaho, Wyoming and Michigan want to get back to the way things were in the good old 1950s. Killing a wolf and taking a "selfie" with the fur that once adorned its body is still an acceptable practice in some quarters. Those quarters are typically dominated by weekend warriors (take another look at the canned hunter on display in the Guardian for the classic "smirk"). Then again American hunters assisted in the near elimination of the America's mascot: the Bald Eagle.

But it is not just Americans that seek the death penalty for the Gray Wolf (or are crushing the biosphere that that supports life on Earth). It is the same story, for example, in France. According to the Telegraph, UK,

"Conservation groups are furious. To return to wolf hunts as if we were in the Middle Ages is scandalous. That the local authorities are organizing them is even worse, said Jean-François Darmstaedter, president of Ferus, who threatened to challenge their

legality in the European courts.

We call them 'political killings' as their only aim is to allow farmers to let off steam but they will solve nothing. Blindly shooting wolves will have no effect other than to exacerbate the problem. If you kill the alpha male, you can split up a pack, which will cause far more damage. The only solution, he said, was to protect flocks properly by using fierce Pyrenean Patou mountain dogs, penning sheep inside high electrified fences at night and firing warning shots if wolves approach. These measures can reduce predation to almost nil, he insisted."

Just Like the Wolves: Humans Negated, Written off, Warehoused, Displaced

There is a statement in the comment section on PBS' *The Wolf that Changed America*. It serves as a brutal reminder of the willingness of humanity to expel through genocide, war, and economic/statistical cleansing many collections of human and non-human beings. Those expulsed rarely have the honor of even being lost to recorded history. America's Native Americans provide an example. "The context omitted by this film [The Wolf that Changed America] is the conquest and colonization of New Mexico by the United States and the subsequent ethnic cleansing of the indigenous Americans to make way for cattle ranching, to which the wolves were a threat. Now we speak of the conservation of the "wilderness" and its wild inhabitants. But why are the human inhabitants denied and negated?"

According to the Internal Displacement Monitoring Center (IDMC), there are nearly 30 million internally displaced people (IDP's) around the globe who are, essentially, homeless. War is a primary cause. Making war is a conscious decision by politicians and military leaders who rarely consider the destructive consequences for the indigenous population, culture and infrastructure. As Sassen has pointed out, expulsions are "made" and war may be the ultimate form of expulsion. For example, America's covert actions in the Syrian civil war and its two invasions of Iraq have contributed significantly to the IDP numbers. Remarkably, as a consequence of US war-making the Christian cultures of Iraq and Syria have nearly vanished.

IDMC notes that IDP's are the result of "conflict, generalized violence, human rights violations and natural hazard-induced disasters. It should be noted that these figures do not include all IDP situations by other causes, such as development projects. Furthermore, while the figures have been presented separately here, our analysis shows that conflict, disasters and resulting displacement have multiple and often overlapping root causes and impacts. Over half of the countries affected by conflict since 1970 were also affected by disaster-induced displacement in the last five years alone. This is an important consideration for those tasked with policy-making, protection and assistance." IDMC reports that there are another 37 million IDP's due to "disasters". The USA accounts for 900,000 of that number. Where do they go?

If You Want a Good Job, Commit a Crime and Go to Prison

The invisible laborers in America's prisons reduce the costs for goods and services offered by many large US corporations. Skilled and captive prison labor is used by business and state governments on a regular basis ostensibly to cover the costs of incarceration. There is irony here: What does it say about a society that allows government and business to hire prisoners rather than employing law abiding citizens who are equal to the task? What's the point of being a "good citizen" when there is little reward in playing by the rules of the State-Corporate designed system of life?

Sassen notes that,

"Mass incarceration has long been present in extreme dictatorships. But today it is emerging as inextricably linked to advanced capitalism…Most of the people who are being incarcerated are also the people who do not have work and from whom work will not be found in our current epoch…today's prisoners in the United States and United Kingdom are increasingly today's version of the surplus laboring population common in the brutal beginnings of modern capitalism…many transnational corporations have set up satellite factories inside prisons…Available evidence suggests that the majority of corporations profiting [in some form] from prison labor [include] Chevron, Bank of America, AT&T, Starbucks and Walmart…the profits of private prisons are represented are represented as a positive addition to a country's GDP even as they are a government cost; in contrast, government run prisons are only represented as government debt."

The State-Corporate Complex consciously makes decisions that "expel" one collective group and incorporates another. According to Sassen, "One familiar example in the West that is both complex and extreme is the expelling of low income workers and the unemployed from government social welfare and health programs, as well as from corporate insurance and unemployment support…These expulsion are made. The instruments for this making range from elementary policies to complex institutions, systems and techniques that require specialized knowledge and intricate organizational formats."

Fight the Power! OK! But Where is It Located?

"People as consumers and workers play a diminished role in the profits of a range of economic sectors… This tells us that our period is not quite like earlier forms of capitalism that thrived on the on the accelerated expansion of prosperous working and middle classes…What is next? Historically the oppressed have often risen against their masters. But today the oppressed have mostly been expelled and survive at a great distance from their "oppressors". Further, the oppressor is increasingly a complex system that combines persons, networks and machines with no obvious center" notes Sassen.

The worst elements of capitalism/globalization are everyone's problem. Destruction of the biosphere and much of human and non-human life, and expulsion from society and the record books is a transnational matter. Someone has to care and someone has to remember. It is no coincidence that wherever on the planet one finds one of the tentacles of the globalized State-Corporate System, Expulsions of every kind take place.

Culling the human herd is, of course, best accomplished through a regional or global conflagration pitting one state, or proxy, versus another. In such a conflict everything "is game" (non-humans too).Thepreeminent warring power on the planet, the United States, is—in a case of acute irony– threatening military action and stiffer economic sanctions on Russia if it proceeds under the "responsibility to protect" doctrine to "save" Russian speakers in Eastern Ukraine. And for good measure the US recently warned China not to look to Russia's annexing of the Crimea as a model for an invasion and occupation of the disputed Diaoyu Islands that Japan claims.

How About a Canned War with Humans?

So is the State-Corporate System. designed and led by the USA, gearing up for a shooting/economic war against both Russia and China? Can you say tactical nuclear weapons? The reality is that there are too many people in the world. A large number of them are a drag on economic performance. Many of them are "old" and blocking opportunities for the young. There simply is not enough work and the State-Corporate System does not want to pay "living wages." Why should they when prison labor is widely available.

Odd that the centenary of World War I takes place in 2014.

Humans can only hope that the mystical deity "God" does not become a reality appearing for its pound of flesh. Worse still would be the appearance of an extraterrestrial species that arrives and demands an accounting of humanity's stewardship of the Earth and the life it supports.

Being expelled from the planet would be quite painful.

+++++

A Soulless, Digitally Concussed Western World

The USA and European Union (EU) continue on their downward trajectory in the 14th year of 21st Century. The perpetual state of war against terror, drugs, immigrants, the press and whistle-blowers moves on uninhibited. Another war, this time named Austerity, is being waged by USA and EU leaders against the middle and lower classes. Youth are particularly hard hit with the average unemployment rate in the EU at 23 percent. In the USA the figure is 17 percent according to the Bureau of Labor Statistics. But never mind that.

Cutting benefits, or, rather, throwing people away, will reduce the unemployment rate and that's good for the economy. Such is the mindset of the financier class as reflected in the comments of Joe LaVorgna, chief economist at Deutsch Bank. He noted that in the USA, 23 percent of the 1.5 million who are losing their unemployment benefits will simply exit the work force, and another 850,000, at the state level, would give up on trying to find employment. LaVorgna stated that the unemployment will drop to 6.7 percent. Yippie!

Isn't Economic Security Supposed to be Part of National Security?

So the middle and lower classes are being wiped out by politicians and finance/business interests that, in the main, control what remains of representative democracy in the USA and the EU. Those powerful interests want nothing less than the purchase of the nation state and all the souls within it. Worse still the elite/upper classes are casting out men, women and children by sanctioning the cutting of the Achilles Tendon of social programs meant to ameliorate unemployment and hunger, and limit the effects of life's unanticipated disasters.

Evens as Austerity works its dark magic, the businesses and their politicians that promise a "new day" can't produce enough jobs to to match civil society's needs.

Where did all the cash go to fund domestic programs? In the USA no mention is made of the trillions of dollars borrowed from social security funds by the US government, or the many trillions of dollars expended on wars and weapons programs, or tax cuts that rob from the poor and give to the rich, or the cash hoarding and outsourcing of jobs by US corporations. But reading the economic news on Reuters as 2014 starts, one would think that an economic recovery—even boom—is on schedule for 2014. But the coverage at Reuters, which is based on US government reports, does not match life on the ground in the USA.

Every day the semi-official organs of the USA (New York Times, Washington Post, Wall Street Journal and **other** mainstream news outlets like Fox, CBS, ABC) run stories of the economic carnage taking place in the USA and EU. Accompanying those reports are false messages of hope in sidebars which state "employment is up, housing sales are up, manufacturing is up and the future is bright." Likewise the exploits (covert and overt) of the American and European national security machinery gets big play, as it should. The blood thirsty civil wars ongoing in Libya, Iraq, Syria, Yemen, Afghanistan, the Sudan's, and Egypt all owe their current states of chaos to the USA's and EU's 21st Century colonial strategies and tactics.

For example: Invading Iraq where now Sunni and Shia slaughter each other (Christians have abandoned or are under assault); forcing the creation of South Sudan simply for oil and military basing purposes to counter China's presence; approving a military coup in Egypt; and supporting psychopathic anti-Assad factions in Syria who relish in all forms of execution. It is interesting to note that in Iran, Jews and Christians (each allowed a seat in Iran's parliament under its constitution) are safer than in most of the countries in Iran's neighborhood.

The pounding of complex national security matters—which has merged with national economic security--into the heads of Americans and Europeans is unprecedented in scope. For example, each month dozens of electronic media outlets bring news of remotely piloted aerial vehicles (RPV's) offing some ten cent rebel in Yemen. Unfortunately, in order to get the bad guy, national security officials say, "we had to kill the entire wedding party." Consider the Cyber version of that: in order to get the bad guy, national security officials say, "we had to sweep up all meta-data and our link analysis identified your computer working within the link net. "You may be innocent but we still have to raid your home and take you to jail." It is a nightmare scenario in which American civilians would be subjected to the jurisprudence of Guantanamo Bay. The precedents are in place.

American security and intelligence failures have forever linked the Boston Marathon and Sandy Hook School with "horror and moral terror," as the line goes in the movie Apocalypse Now. With the USA still officially a nation at war and operating under a state of emergency since September, 2001, it is no wonder that Americans have made friends with "horror and moral terror".

Nowhere is that more evident than in the "Breaking Bad" capitalism that both the USA and EU are openly pushing on their populations; they seek the same in the Ukraine, even Russia. The presence of US officials at the site of demonstrations in the Ukraine show the extent to which the US is actively engaged in destabilizing governments friendly to Russia. According to the Christian Science Monitor, "Victoria Nuland, US Assistant Secretary of State, offered cookies and bread to pro-EU activists as she and US Ambassador Geoffrey Pyatt walked through Independence Square in Kiev [Ukraine]..."

Cold War warriors (neoconservatives and neoliberals) were clearly not satisfied with the USSR's collapse. They wanted, and still long for, Russia proper: its land/resources, infrastructure, and human capital. By ringing Russia with missile defense systems, which can be converted to offensive uses for targeting, the USA/EU continue their warring ways. Without President Putin, who knows what Russia would be like. As it is, he has managed to keep his nation state intact in spite of psychopathic fundamentalists, hiding behind Islam, who recently engaged in the killing of civilians in Volgograd. It must irk Putin to no end to know that the USA/EU instigated for the creation of Islamic fundamentalists during the Cold War to fight the "Godless" USSR. It appears that is continuing today with the help of Saudi Arabia.

The USA's Pivot to Asia is more of the same. The USA is prepping for war in Asia, the site of 60 percent of the world's population. It is a dangerous US national security strategy only profitable for arms manufacturers and transnational business interests.

Austerity means squeezing the life and profit out of many millions in the middle and lower income classes in the USA and EU. Workers in both assemblages and classes were once silently content to labor 40 hours in a week—maybe a few more-- with health insurance benefits and some paid holidays. Now they are anxiously looking over their shoulders. It is not enough any longer to work hard, pay the bills on time, and have two days off during each work week. The vaunted middle class so prized by every national economy on the planet is fading. There is no longer Economic Security; in fact, there is no security at all.

Making Matters Worse:Digitally Concussed

The USA and EU adoption of a sort of Meth-based Capitalism has far greater consequences thanks to the Internet/WWW and the mobile communications revolution. If one carries a mobile device or uses a laptop, one can be found, fixed and targeted, even scooped up as collateral damage. God—in the form of a security-military-capitalist dynamic, is watching.

It is a return to the Medieval Consciousness (from *Obama of the Digital Inquisition by John Stanton*):

"Christ stated that "God works in mysterious ways. Who else do you think controls the electromagnetic spectrum, gravity, thermodynamics, synapses, neurons. You can call God the NSA, CIA, PRISM, Big Data, Tempora or whatever silly name you want, but that's just evidence of God's good work. You all have made the human mind more susceptible to His will than at anytime in humanity's existence. God thinks; no, He knows that the vast majority of citizens in the Holy American Judeo-Christian Empire will set aside their individuality and this 'nonsense called free will' and henceforth, in a blessed moment of uncertainty, ask Is God-NSA listening in? Can God see me when I am sleeping? Can God see my anti-God dreams (punishable, of course)? Oh what joyful compliance will ensue when war and austerity are the

norm!"

There are no boundaries or balance between public and private space. The notion of solitude, of an impenetrable private space for contemplation, or even talking with one's God, has been overwritten by the need to feel part of a digital collective. Such membership eliminates the work effort required to go out in the community and participate in collective action where all manner of human motions, emotions and senses are encountered. Of course, all participants in the digital collective can be surveilled, tracked with ease. In a sense, their unseen digital masters/influencers are the Gods and Angels of the Cyber world ensuring that one's life is filled with product placement advertisements, advice on this and that emotional problem, and thoughtless information and mind-numbing, violent video games. Digital denizens have put their faith not so much in the machines as in the humans who control the machinery of the Internet and program the content that appears on the World Wide Web.

The digital collective is a sterile thing. Individuals lose their consciousness and memory of life on the other side while in Cyber space. The news of the day, the workplace, the children, the bills are all one big blur. But the Internet machines provide access to the World Wide Web and there is where one finds peace away from the gritty, mundane life outside of Cyber space, and where the world is crystal clear, quiet and there is no face-to-face human contact.. It is as if the digital denizens have suffered some sort of concussion—a sort of digital concussion that jolts portions of the brain, removing empathy; thought and memory of the handshake; the challenge of face-to-face interpersonal relations; the necessity of vigilance in watching the overlords of society; getting out into slums to help the poor; and, more to the point, taking the chance to find the soul, and a contemplative space not in the I-Phone (a machine), but in the lively and colorful world. In short, the fear of solitude and privacy, or being alone in thought, is in the ascendancy. One is never alone when connected to the Internet/WWW.

Soldiers: Pope Francis and Malcolm X

The Apostolic Exhortation, Evangelli Guadium of the Holy Father Francis, lays out the darkness of USA/EU culture, governance and its brand of Capitalism. In a time gone by Malcolm X said much the same. In his closing statement at the Oxford Union in 1964 he maintained that "when one is moderate in the pursuit of justice for human beings, I say he is a sinner....And in my opinion the young generation of whites, blacks, browns, and whatever else there is, your are living in a time when there has to be a change...a better world needs to be built...And I will join in with anyone, I don't what color he is, as long as he wants to change the miserable condition that exists on this earth."

The former big-city bouncer, and the first Jesuit Pope, channels some of Malcolm X. In doing Pope Francis is being true to the missionary history of his order in taking to task the soulless, brain damaged human capital in the USA and EU. These damaged human beings—those who lead and the blind who follow--are the products of 13 years of global conflict, class war, propaganda, greed and exploitation of every conceivable kind. The Pope's message was desperately needed and is a universal one that transcends the garb of religion--Catholic, Muslim or Buddhist. As Malcolm X said, "it is simply a matter of justice for [fellow] human beings."

As a Jesuit Soldier of Jesus, Pope Francis is well aware that the quest for a better world will be a long and difficult struggle. His training prepared him for the campaign. Loyola, the founder of the Jesuit order, was a former military commander. It is no surprise that the Jesuits are sometimes referred to as the US Marine Corps of the Catholic Church, or that Pope Francis used a military metaphor in his Exhortation "...*fervor is replaced by the empty pleasure of complacency and self-indulgence. This way of thinking also feeds the vainglory of those who are content to have a modicum of power and would rather be the general of a defeated army than a mere private in a unit which continues to fight.*"

Pope Francis would seem to have enough to do in cleaning up the many well publicized troubles in his organization. He also has to convince some 1 billion-plus followers to stick with the Catholic

Church. Even with all that on his plate, this Jesuit, this soldier, is compelled by his order to build a better world, not just a better religion. That's a transcendent goal really. It requires souls filled with passion for the world and life. Is a God really needed for that to be achieved? Many believe so.

As Malcolm X said "it is simply a matter of justice for [fellow] human beings." That's a religion isn't it?

Excerpts from Pope Francis' Exhortation: "*Our world is being torn apart by wars and violence, and wounded by a widespread individualism which divides human beings, setting them against one another as they pursue their own well-being. In various countries, conflicts and old divisions from the past are re-emerging...The current financial crisis can make us overlook the fact that it originated in a profound human crisis: the denial of the primacy of the human person! We have created new idols. The worship of the ancient golden calf has returned in a new and ruthless guise in the idolatry of money and the dictatorship of an impersonal economy lacking a truly human purpose. The worldwide crisis affecting finance and the economy lays bare their imbalances and, above all, their lack of real concern for human beings; man is reduced to one of his needs alone: consumption.*

The need to resolve the structural causes of poverty cannot be delayed, not only for the pragmatic reason of its urgency for the good order of society, but because society needs to be cured of a sickness which is weakening and frustrating it, and which can only lead to new crises. Welfare projects, which meet certain urgent needs, should be considered merely temporary responses. As long as the problems of the poor are not radically resolved by rejecting the absolute autonomy of markets and financial speculation and by attacking the structural causes of inequality, no solution will be found for the world's problems or, for that matter, to any problems. Inequality is the root of social ills.

The dignity of each human person and the pursuit of the common good are concerns which ought to shape all economic policies. At times, however, they seem to be a mere addendum imported from without in order to fill out a political discourse lacking in .perspectives or plans for true and integral development. How many words prove irksome to this system! It is irksome when the question of ethics is raised, when global solidarity is invoked, when the distribution of goods is mentioned, when reference in made to protecting labor and defending the dignity of the powerless...Casual indifference in the face of such questions empties our lives and our words of all meaning."

+++++

Antidotes to Cyber Industrialization and the Swarm Culture

Get the cure before you become part of the swarm.

Antidote #1: The People's Platform: Taking Back Power and Culture in the Digital Age, Astra Taylor, Metropolitan Books, 2014.

Antidote #2: The Massachusetts Institute of Technology Press' Semiotext(e) Intervention Series: Factories of Knowledge, Industries of Creativity, Gerald Raunig; The Uprising: On Poetry and Finance, Franco Bernardi; Theory of the Young Girl, Tiqqun; and The Agony of Power, Jean Baudrillard.

Antidote #3: Global Interdependence--The World After 1945 (Volume 6); A World Connecting, 1870-1945 (Volume 5), General Editors Akira Iriye and Jurgen Osterhamme.

"A network is a plurality of organic and artificial beings of humans and machines who perform continuous actions thanks to procedures that make possible their interconnection and interpretation. If you do not adapt to these procedures, if you don't follow the technical rules of the games, you are not playing the game. If you don't react to certain stimuli in the programmed way you don't form part of the network. The behavior of persons in a network is not aleatory because the network implies and predisposes pathways for the networked.

A swarm is a plurality of living beings whose behavior follows (or seems to follow) rules embedded in their neural systems. Biologists call a swarm a multitude of animals of similar size and bodily orientation moving together in the same direction and performing actions in a coordinated way....In conditions of social Hypercomplexity human beings tend to act like a swarm. When the Info-sphere is too dense and too fast for conscious elaboration of information, people tend to conform to shared behavior...In a broader sense we may say that in the digital age power is about making things easy. In a Hypercomplex environment that cannot be properly understood and governed by the individual mind, people will follow simplified pathways and will use complexity reducing machines.

This is why social behavior today seems to be trapped in regular and inescapable patterns of interaction. Geolinguistics procedures, financial obligations, social needs and Pyschomedia invasion: all this machinery is framing the field of the possible and incorporating common cognitive processes in the behavior of social actors. In a swarm it is not impossible to say no. But it is irrelevant. You can express your refusal, your rebellion but it is not going to change the direction of the swarm nor is it going to affect the way the swarm's brain is elaborating information." (Bernardi)

If everybody jumped off a bridge, would you too? In the future human beings may not even be cognizant of having jumped off a bridge or understand why they think and act the way they do.

The "bridge jump" line is one of the favored of parent's when dealing with their offspring who want to follow the pack. "Think", the parents say. "Look before you leap!" The advice is sound, of course, and the point is that there is, or should be, a conscious, contemplative and critical choice that the youngster can make: run with the pack and court trouble or break away. This is time tested advice that both today's youth and adults seem to forget.

The key words here are conscious, contemplative, critical and choice. The words and concepts they represent are disappearing in today's overhyped 21st Century. The Cyber/virtual swarm is advancing rapidly and is absorbing and re-territorializing the human brain, altering hand-to-hand human activity. The scene from Star Ship Troopers in which "the bug" sucks up a human brain is an apt metaphor. What is a hive but a machine?

The theology of the moment in many parts of the globe is the faith and belief in the development and realization of a sort of technologically driven Nirvana where everyone and everything will be connected and interconnected via the Internet, World Wide Web and mobile devices. Interdependencies will check and save us all.

It is believed and proclaimed by the high priests at Microsoft, Google, Oracle, Wall Street--and US government technocrats--that ubiquitous and globalized high speed communications are humanity's salvation. To shareholders they promise an endless stream of profit; to the general public the environmental friendliness of technology over paper; to the oppressed of the world the development of a middle and youth-class with some measure of human security; to artists dictatorial creative freedom; and to women and minorities the shattering of wage inequality. All one individual or collective need do is broadcast on Twitter and, just like the Disney slogan goes, "dreams can come true, it can happen to you."

That's not happening for women and minorities though, particularly in the world of the techno-priesthood. According to Astra Taylor--author of the People's Platform, "Over 85 percent of venture capitalists are men looking to invest in other men and women make forty-nine cents for every dollar their male counterparts rake in. Though 40 percent of private businesses are women-owned, nationwide only 8 percent of the venture-backed tech start-ups are. Established companies are equally segregated. The National Center for Women and Information Technology reports that of the top 100 tech companies, only 6 percent of chief executives are women. The numbers for Asians who ascend to the top are comparable despite the fact that they make up a third of all Silicon Valley software engineers. In 2010 not even 1 percent of the founders of Silicon Valley companies were black..."

Mountains of E-Waste on the Ground

The sales pitch by technocrats, venture capitalists, financiers, engineers, politicians and alternative media is far more suspect, complex, violent and environmentally unsound than they, and the New and Mainstream Media. care to publicize. They keep a close hold on the fact that a public internet does not exist and that purity drives the manufacture of the communications infrastructure.

As Taylor points out "There is no such thing as a public internet: everything flows through private pipes …The weightless rhetoric of digital technology masks a refusal to acknowledge the people and resources on which these systems depend: lithium and coltan mines, energy-guzzling data centers and server farms, suicidal workers at Apple's Foxconn factories, and women and children in developing countries and incarcerated Americans up to their necks in toxic electronic waste…It is estimated that mining the gold necessary to produce a single cell phone—only one mineral of many required for the finished product—produces upwards of 220 pounds of waste…In the United States data centers account for approximately 2 percent of the country's energy consumption and climbing with each center guzzling as much electricity as a small town and the power overwhelmingly provided by the burning of coal, a cheap but filthy fuel source.

And so our mountains of e-waste grow three times faster than the piles of regular garbage accumulating all around us. Hundreds of millions of still-functioning gadgets—billions of pounds of hazardous waste-leaching stuff, are thrown away every year,….By 2005 there were already more than half a billion outmoded mobile phones tucked away in American desk drawers."

The 21st Century Gods of the Anthropocence at Apple, Verizon, Goldman Sachs, the Wall Street Journal and the Office of the US President make feeble attempts to dip their toes into the mixed history of technological wizardry like railroads, the telegraph and undersea cables. No private or public concern wants to talk about the grimy backdrop to it all. The awful reality of pulling the globe together in the 1800's, for example, was the destruction of localities rich in plant life and, sometimes, indigenous peoples and their languages and cultures. All of which was wiped out for the sake of a 60 second telegraph message. Today the value of destruction is a 15 second "text".

"As entrepreneurs raced to lay oceanic telegraphic cables during the second half of the 19th Century, the demand rose sharply for a natural rubber like substance called gutta-percha which could protect electric lines from sweater corrosion. Found in Southeast Asia…the gutta-percha boom deforested land and changed the power of relationships and living patterns of nearby people. This ravaging of specific Southeast Asian forestland enabled both a European centered revolution and also a global network of connectivity. It helped draw people together even as it created inequalities. Thinking simultaneously about the forest dwellers living locally and the near instantaneous telegraphy which obliterated space and time helps suggest the many unpredictable relationships within this era's local, national, imperial, international and transnational networks of people, goods and ideas…Such networked processes epitomize the invisible and irregular currents of global change within transitional space during this period and they foreshadow the complexities of power that would characterized the late 20th Century and beyond."

Techno-Corporations Shaping the Environment of the Individual and Global Mind

The Pentagon and the National Security Agency are pilloried for designing and executing doctrine that seeks to shape and alter the geopolitical landscape in favor of US interests, whether in or out of cyberspace. These national security precedents are located in so many words in the Constitution of the United States.

President Obama, just like every other prior American president, has been very clear about how the United States will use its instruments of national power (diplomatic, informational, military, economic, financial, law enforcement, intelligence and its people) to ensure the country's preeminence on the planet no matter who or what gets in the way. "The United States will protect its people and advance our prosperity irrespective of the actions of any other nation…"

In short the US national security apparatus states very publicly, and in readily available policy and doctrinal online documents, exactly what they intend and, in the main, how they are going implement strategy and tactics (for example the President's National Security Strategy and the Pentagon's National Military Strategy). That's not the case with Facebook, Yahoo, or AT&T and their legions of marketers, propagandists and hired academics.

Their policy, doctrine and user data/trends are all labeled "corporate proprietary" even as they seek to manipulate individual and collective consumers through marketing practices (now based on the latest neuroscience) to adopt the latest Techno-corporations appropriate consumer data from nearly every segment of the US economy to include the massive K-16 education industry. They are nearly omnipresent via television, radio, webpages, mobile devices, newspapers, billboards, the supermarket shopping aisle, clothing, sponsorships, credit reports, music sales and word-of-mouth. Their logos also appear on race cars, sail boats, stadiums, high school score boards and professional sports uniforms. They make the Pentagon/NSA full spectrum dominance notion look silly.

The 21st Century Cyber Magnates have built on practices and visions based on 19th and early 20th Century corporate and industrialist practices endorsed by both representative and fascist governments alike and an enthralled and fascinated public. There is a key difference though: Cyber Industrialists now have the manipulative neuroscientific tools and the medium to go far beyond the dismal education of the past to legitimize the clearing of forests, the pollution the oceans, and the suppression and mechanization of creativity and ideas.

The 21st Century Robber Barons/Mind Thieves now have the technological, social and financial capital to clear-cut axons, dendrites, neurons, genes and, consequently, conscious life to make way for global conformity/obedience and consumption…"the function of creative factories consists not only of the mechanized manufacture of entertainment goods but also [for] controlling experience, consumption, reproduction….and [the creation] total ambivalence [to it all]…Baudrillard, Raunig

"I'm so happy I could give a shit about being free!" (Tiqqun)

+++++

Ukraine's Leaders Seek National Socialism and Dictatorship:

Americanization and Liberalism are Poison

So the US leadership is supporting the creation of One Nation Under God in Ukraine. As one of the key groups involved in the militant overthrow of an elected government has stated in its party platform, "a system of the dictatorship of the Nation with regard to the socioeconomic interests of the people" needs to be implemented (more below).

Isn't that what the military in Egypt proclaimed in its coup to oust another elected official, Morsi?

The American press is fond of patting itself on the back for upholding the first amendment to the US Constitution, that being, among other things, freedom of the press. But that does not mean the freedom to obfuscate, ignore facts and curry favor with the US national security apparatus in whatever covert or overt form it takes.

The New York Times, Wall Street Journal and the Washington Post have engaged, once again, in a classic information operations effort on behalf of dangerous. Special interests. This time it is to shape a national anti-Russian consensus to mock the legitimate concerns of the Russian government: US military expansion and attempts to incite regime change in Russia.

The power of the three media outlets exists in the corporate, for-profit nature of the enterprises, not any notable journalistic enterprise. They engage in pay-for-journalism beholden to advertisers, shareholders, investors and the US government. All three groups are known to collaborate on stories with state, local and federal officials so that news is not news to officialdom. But as Don Corleone said in the movie The Godfather, "It's just business." What else can one expect from a quasi-representative democracy?

The Wall Street Journal is owned by Fox News Corporation. News Corporation's ability to reach into and shape the opinions of tens of millions of the global watching/listening public is unprecedented. From the Wall Street Journal to National Geographic--and hundreds of media outlets local, national and global--it can carry its anti-Russian message 24 hours a day, 7 days a week.

The Washington Post is owned by Jeff Bezos of Amazon fame. Little reported is the $600 million contract it recently won to provide the CIA with information technology products and services. Bezos had negligible presence in Washington, DC prior to his acquisition of the Washington Post, but now has a very loud voice. The Post has always been close to the CIA and other national security agencies with Katherine Graham (former owner) indicating in a speech to the CIA that there are some things Americans "don't need to know and should not..."

That might have been the case decades ago, but in the age of the Internet/WWW, hackers and independent journalists who know "it's not about the money" and can report freely, Graham's statement is nonsense. In short, in 2014 the playbook of the ruling class is open for all to see.

And what of the dreary New York Times? Gray indeed. This just about sums up what a once great journalistic enterprise has become. *"Now in its fourteenth year the Luxury Conference is one of the world's most prestigious annual forums for the global luxury business, bringing together 500+ of the most senior business and creative leaders from the top echelons of the industry to gain insights, share ideas and expand their international networks. The 2013 conference took place in Singapore and examined the growing influence of Southeast Asia in the luxury market - as both creator and consumer. Speakers included: Ermenegildo Zegna; Domenico De Sole, President, Tom Ford International; Angelica Cheung, Editor in Chief, Vogue China; Anna Sui, Founder, Anna Sui; Bryan Grey Yambao, Blogger, bryanboy.com; HRH Princess Marie-Chantal, Founder and Creative Director, Marie-Chantal; and Andrew Keith, President, Lane Crawford and Joyce The award-winning 2012 conference took place in Rome and analyzed the potential of Africa and the power of the Mediterranean with contributions from major names such as Bono, Donatella Versace, Jean-Paul Gaultier and Vivienne Westwood."*

But no matter.

Dean Acheson once said that Americans could hold focus on

international issues for about ten minutes. So maybe President Obama is doing Americans a service by cutting back on press freedom. But wait! Isn't that something that President Putin would do?

One Nation Under God in Ukraine

Party Platform of UNA-UNSO. Note the logo for the party.

"Required: Terminate the current practice of destroying the education system through its Americanization and privatization...*National Social Power*--a system of the dictatorship of the Nation with regard to the socio economic interests of the people..Our enemies: communism, cosmopolitanism, liberalism

God created us in Ukrainian and Hallowed be His will for evermore. We stand for God's will. God is with us! Our highest duty: the implementation of Ukrainian national idea - the idea of self-assertion of the Nation, the creation of the state of the Ukrainian national system...the purpose of the education system must be to develop the creative potential of the nation, the formation of highly educated personnel, education nationally conscious, active, selfless and sacrificial citizens of Ukraine."

Party Platform of Right Sector. Note the Logo for the party.

"The purpose of human existence is [to be] closer to God - or man, society, state degraded, degenerate and decadent. Humanists its [their] struggle with Christianity began with the denial of God and the deification of man: Man Anthem! Man, not God (P.Tychyna). Because of Jacobinism, socialism and social democracy, they naturally came to National Socialism, which turned man into beast, and communism that worked meaningless servants and destroyed millions of oppressed peoples. The current through demoliberalizm (sic) humanists, cosmopolitanism and globalization are not only individuals but entire countries are by atheism and denationalization, homosexuality and drug addiction.

Christ's teaching comes to everyone. And the man has to take care that the grain of truth zakorenylysya and sprouted in her soul a living faith. The child must grow and protect. Faith must cultivate and protect. Bandera [Nazi collaborator] taught: "We need not distinguish the defense of the Christian faith and the Church of the national liberation struggle, just concentrate and focus the main efforts around those critical statements against which the enemy directs strongest attack..Head over to the school between young children, where the enemy is trying to fill their hearts with Moscow and Washington poison, and taught there will be love and devotion to his native land."

Party Platform of Svoboda

"Svoboda's nationalism is based on love, respect, and honour...We are Social Nationalists. We do neither belong to the old Communist nor to the new Democratic nomenclature. We have a new vision of the world and we can correctly assess the political developments in Ukraine.

Set the graph "nationality" in the passport and birth certificate. Determine the nationality by birth certificate or birth certificate of the parents, considering the requests of the citizen...Implement a criminal penalty for any displays of Ukrainophobia...Implement a "Reproductive Health of the Nation" program. Disallow abortion except due to medical issues, and/or rape, which were proved in court. Align the implementation of illegal abortion to attempted murder in the criminal law."

+++++

America's Deep State Waging Absurd Wars: American Kids and the World Pay the Price

Could there be any connection between the size of those corporate profits and Washington's patriotic dedication to eternal warfare? That great transfer of wealth helps explain how the gap between rich and poor in America has become and ever widening canyon. The financial dynamics of war-making are rarely mentioned in connection with America's woes but from the profiteer's point of view widening income inequality might be seen as a contribution to national security. During the past 12 year of wars defined from the start as endless the ranks of the poor have increased exponentially while public services like the education system that once enable them to rise have decayed ensuring that a supply of deluded kids impoverished in every way will don the uniforms of soldiers and perform the next round of America's unnecessary wars….Corporations bring home the bacon, soldiers only medals." They Were Soldiers, Ann Jones, Haymarket Books (2013)

"'Nothing in my experience prepared me for the catastrophic nature of these injuries.' His first surgical patient three days after he arrived at Bagram was a young soldier who had stepped on an IED triggering an upward blast that destroyed his legs and left his pelvic cavity hollowed out. His urinary system was in shreds. His testicles were destroyed. His penis was attached to his body by only a little thread of skin…To have to amputate that boy's penis and watch it go into the surgical waste container—it was so emotional.'" They Were Soldiers, Ann Jones, Haymarket Books (2013)

Ann Jones' They Were Soldiers is the Johnny Got His Gun (Dalton Trumbo, 1938) of the 21st Century. Brilliantly and systematically written, Jones' book is an indictment of politicians, military leaders, corporations and the academic/medical communities and their collective complicity in destroying America's middle/lower classes and in particular America's "kids" both male and female alike. What kind of nation and what kind of people promote such insanity, even glorifying current wars in the hopes that more war can prosecuted?

After reading They Were Soldiers, which is a book about the fate of male and female soldiers who return home broken, mangled and raped, the realization strikes that without perpetual overt and covert war, the American system of governance—as it is now practiced--would collapse. That is a frightening thought. Moreover, America's elite class blames everyone but themselves for the ungluing and subsequent militarization of American society. They, according to one US Army official interviewed by Jones, are con-artists and hucksters. They prey upon youth.

Absurdist USA

"I've been in the Army twenty-six years and I can tell you it's a con." Jones says he doesn't think much of military bosses or politicians or Americans in general who send the lowliest one percent to make the one percent on the high end "monufuckinmentally rich." Jones says that the Army official has two sons, 21 and 23, in college. "They won't have to serve. Before that happens I'll shoot them myself...War is absurd. Boys don't know any better. But for a grown man to be trapped in stupid wars--it's embarrassing, it's humiliating, and it is absurd."

The American horror story begins with the propaganda that Americans have created and love to bathe in. That propaganda includes notions such as war fighting is noble and glorious; America takes care of its "fallen soldiers", America is the guarantor and protector of the world's freedom; soldiers and contractors, fighting side-by-side, protect the US Constitution; America is the "land of the free and home of the brave." American "kids" in the 21st Century are heavily indoctrinated into a national security culture in which more is known about weaponry and war than literature and critical thinking.

According to Jones, one veteran of the Iraq war campaign asked himself, "Why did I like carrying an M-16? I waited in line with the others in Basic Training like it was Christmas morning...I was elated to receive the famous M-16. All the movies and video games never showed me what it truly was. During my time in the Army I finally understood what a rifle was all about. It's a tool of death...I have to be honest. I loved carrying a rifle...After a while it is fused into my skin, bones character and soul...I came from an average all-American family. My mom is a schoolteacher. Our walls are filled with weddings. I open doors for little old ladies...If I am a normal middle-class kid, then something is wrong. Why did I know the difference between an M-16 and an AK-47 before I could compare a Hindu to a Muslim, or a Sonnet to a Haiku?"

Ghastly Leadership: Loves to Hate Women

After so many years of war, American culture is arguably borderline paranoiac, if not outright. Jones points out in her book that the USA is the only culture-nation in the world always looking for a fight. American culture—particularly those who make up the elite class--stinks of irresponsibility and non-accountability. Not convinced? Who in the USA stood accountable for the intelligence failures of 911? How about the senseless blunder of the Iraq and Afghanistan wars? How about the intelligence/police shenanigans and dismal security that led to the Boston Marathon Bombings? Then there is Benghazi Massacre, the Great Recession of 2008, the ruse of health care for all pushed by the Obama administration and its corporate sponsors. Only in America could such a ghastly elite/class absolve itself of responsibility. And yet they promote themselves to higher ranks even though lives and wars are lost. They are reelected again and again for taking America to ruin.

The disdain with which America's Political-Military-Corporate-Academic Elite treat male and female soldiers (and US civilians too) is criminal. Nowhere is this more evident than in the treatment of soldiers who return from America's many wars both large (Iraq and Afghanistan) and small (drug wars in South America, terror wars on the African continent). The US government/military largely dispenses with those soldiers who have "invisible" injuries such as trauma, depression, panic and anxiety caused by the external experience of death, wounding or rape which, in turn, becomes internalized, part of the soul. The soldiers return with nearly no support base to traumatize families and communities, sometimes by murdering relatives or strangers. Women are the target of much of this aggression which displays itself before the homicide takes place.

Commanders have routinely condoned the "rough" treatment of women making the environment for rape and other sexual misconduct a friendly one. Real men slap women around seems to be the unwritten rule in the military ranks. One commander in Iraq told Jones that he was happy that US women soldiers were in his command because "the Afghan women are dogs." The implications of that statement are clear.

In another instance the US military tried to downplay a string of murders perpetrated by soldiers stationed at Fort Carson, Colorado. "Only after the ninth homicide at Fort Carson did the Army start a local inquiry into the murders," writes Jones. "The general in charge said they were 'looking for a trend among the homicidal soldiers. Something happened through their life cycle that might have contributed to this.' An Army prosecutor asked,

'Where is this aggression coming from.'"

No mention is made of the fact that these "kids" were trained to kill and that the US political and military establishment doesn't give a damn—beyond lip service--about their reintegration into American society.

Sometimes the military dumps the injured men and women quickly back into civilian care before they can complete a process that qualifies them for government benefits. Mostly, benefits or not, they end up with a cart full of prescriptions ranging from Zoloft to Oxycontin prescribed by government contracted doctors in the Veterans Administration and assorted medical facilities on US military bases around the world. Pharmaceutical corporations know that perpetual war and the propaganda of fear are great for business.

Noonan's Deep State (she knows about Turkey's experience)

The effect of 12 years of war against ghostly enemies has distorted American culture bringing it to the doorstep of fascism. The silent war of surveillance (exposed by Edward Snowden) that is being waged by the elite class of America against American citizens and independent journalists/whistleblowers is evidence of that. Peggy Noonan writing in the Wall Street Journal alludes to a secretive Deep State in America that likes war and subterfuge. "I have come increasingly to think of as the deep state—again, the vast, unfathomable and not fully accountable innards of the permanent U.S. intelligence and national-security apparatus…the ways, needs, demands, imperatives, secrets and strategies…stay pretty much the same, except for one thing: They always want more. The dynamic is always toward growth, toward more reach and more power."

To increase power, to silence critics is a tool of the Deep State. Returning soldiers are subject to its will too. Many US soldiers—male and female--have come to bear a "moral revulsion" for the actions of the USA in the premeditated destruction of the planet's cultures and nations. They must be silenced.

"A Marine veteran of Iraq and Afghanistan told me that a Veterans Affairs therapist labeled her with Post Traumatic Stress

Disorder though she had neither experienced nor complained of a traumatic event. Instead she had spoken of feeling a kind of moral revulsion from life in the US after seeing how people in the rest of the world live.

Many returned soldiers have that same feeling coupled with a smoldering rage at having lost the lives that once, in their innocence, would have contented them—the family trips to Walmart and the Happy Meals at McDonald's with all the kids. That's a world they can't fit into anymore because as the Marine veteran said. 'We've seen the price the world pays for the American Way of Life.' They are unable to resume their old lives not because of injury or trauma, though that's part of it for some, but because they know too much.

She said, 'Try to get a little help for hypervigilance and the VA hands you a medical diagnosis and a bunch of prescriptions to shut you up. We've seen a lot and learned things Americans ought to know. But we are the last people they want to be on the loose—the 'crazy vets of Vietnam back again.'"

+++++

Welcome to Whitehead's Cannibal War Machine: 21ˢᵗ Century Hell

"At the same time the progressive evacuation in the 20th century of the nation-state as a means of class domination and the advent of a nomadic pirate class of financial capital, means that the practice of endemic global war has become indifferent to national territory and so functionally infinite in its horizons for future conflict The cannibal war-machine thus consumes persons and ecologies through forms of commodity production and price speculation that profit from the systematic creation of social chaos and its re-ordering through the violence and destruction of high-tech military performance and the enforced disciplines of emergency or pandemic management and homeland security...And this mystique is consciously promoted by military and police world-wide, entering a global cultural imaginary that ceaselessly replays the violent performances of both military and insurgent, police and criminal, Such virtual experiences circulate incessantly through

electronic media whose consumption mesmerizes, stupefies and enchains individual subjectivities to The Cannibal War Machine."
Neil Whitehead, Divine Hunger

Sad that Neil Whitehead is not around to provide insights into the machinations underway from Ukraine to Syria. He'd likely point out that the world can't focus solely on the Holy Wars underway in Eurasia and that the Divine Cannibal War Machine is on the move-in some fashion-on every continent. Indeed it is.

It is increasingly difficult to stomach the propaganda and demonization of a bunch of nihilists wearing the mask of Islam by a bunch of destructive capitalists wearing the mask of Christianity (or should we say the mask of Judaism since the destructive capitalists have stood by as Christians in the Middle East are purged and displaced). The nihilists and the destructive capitalists are flip-sides of Janus-faced Saudi Arabia and its vile Wahhabi, capitalist-influenced doctrine. All three groupings are distinguished by their psychopathic and sociopathic leadership that views the bulk of humanity as non-recyclable material.

For those Americans mesmerized into supporting another US military invasion of Iraq-to include Syria-to bring peace and love to the region, take a look at the US homeland where citizens in Detroit are deemed to have "no fundamental right to water". There are millions of Americans (including US military Veterans) who are homeless and impoverished. The economy is not recovering unless one thinks that thousands of newly created part-time service industry work, with no benefits, is the sign of an economy on the rise. The actor Jeff Daniels in HBO's The Newsroom sums up the dire situation in the USA better than any "reality" American news reader, academic, politician, flag officer or pundit. What does it say when the actor playing a part is more believable than the "real" experts and leaders?

Cannibals Leave a Legacy

The world has been inundated with videos of the Islamic Caliphate removing the heads of Westerners fool hardy enough to think that they have a right to life, liberty and the pursuit of happiness in the brutality of a war zone. They receive a hero's funeral in the global mainstream media and are lauded for their humanitarianism on behalf of the "civilized" world.

Let's take a look at some of the activity of the "civilized" Divine Cannibal War Machine and see if it reaches the level of horror that the Islamic Caliphate is charged with. First up, the legacy of the US military's use of the defoliant Agent Orange in Vietnam. The UK Daily Mail has a photo essay on the matter that deals with birth defects caused by the lingering effect of the toxin. The report was published in April of 2014: "A new series of heartbreaking pictures has revealed even babies 40 years on are suffering the horrific effects of Agent Orange in Vietnam. Canterbury born Francis Wade captured the distressing images at the Thi Nghe and Thien Phuoc orphanages in Saigon, which are home to children born decades after the war. Yet despite the conflict ending in 1971, the orphanages are caring for children suffering disabilities thought to be caused by a chemical used by U.S forces, which was sprayed on crops, plants and trees."

According to the Vietnam Veterans Association, "Agent Orange was a combination of two defoliants, 2-4-5-T and 2-4-D contaminated by dioxin (TCDD), a toxic byproduct of the chemical production process. More than 19 million gallons of herbicides were sprayed in Vietnam between 1962 and 1971. More than 11.2 million gallons sprayed after 1965 were dioxin-contaminated Agent Orange. Agents Purple, Pink, and Green used before 1965 were even more highly contaminated with dioxin. "My father passed away in 1998. He had many health problems, including type II diabetes. He was only 50 years old. Agent Orange has been a part of my life from the moment I was born. I was born without my right leg, several of my fingers, and my big toe on my left foot. My mother had three miscarriages. My younger brother (age 29) has to wear bifocals and suffers from chronic joint pain."

You Don't Need Your Life or that Pinkey Finger

The Stanford Daily offers a critical view of the documentary The

Kill Team based on the murder, by American soldiers, of three Afghan nationals unlucky enough to have encountered thugs masquerading as uniformed soldiers. The film reviewer notes wryly that in such instances, the US military uses the "few bad apples" clause to indicate that the murder and mutilation of civilians is just a hiccup and not part of the indoctrination that seeks to teach humans to kill without consciousness. It's the same mentality that was at work during the My Lai Massacre and other mass killings undertaken by US military/contractor personnel in Vietnam.

"Murder victims included a disabled man, an Islamic mullah and a 15-year old boy, Gul Mudin, who was working on his father's farm. American soldiers stripped Mudin's corpse, severed the boy's pinky finger as a trophy and posed for photos with his mutilated body. Krauss makes no move to explore the effects of these killings on Afghan communities.... Following the Maywand District murders, government officials portrayed the atrocities as the product of a few bad apples rather than systemic issues within the armed forces. It is laudable that director Dan Krauss sought to interrogate, or at least contextualize, this framing of the crimes. In all likelihood, there is a documentary to be made about the institutional conditions and leadership vacuum that made the crimes possible. But "The Kill Team" is not that movie."

"You Might Say He Lost His Head" (Austin Powers)

In 1994 a soldier in the US Army cut off a fellow soldier's head for sleeping with his wife. The infuriated married man then took his comrade's head to the hospital where is wife was resting in expectation of giving birth to a child. The miffed red-blooded American husband placed the head on her bedroom nightstand and left. At any rate, Saudi Arabia has beheaded 54 humans thus far in 2014, according to NDTV. Two of the crimes include witchcraft and drug trafficking. There is an upside to beheading as opposed to being vaporized by an atom bomb (Hiroshima, Nagasaki) or Hellfire missile: There is evidence to suggest that when the head is cut off consciousness remains for some length of time. "...the brain can continue to produce thoughts and experience sensations for at least several seconds following decapitation -- in rats, at least. Although findings in rats are commonly extrapolated onto humans, we may never fully know if a human remains similarly conscious after the head is lost. As author Alan Bellows points out, 'Further scientific observation of human decapitation is unlikely.'"

While Americans are not fond of beheadings-that'd be too much work for lazy Americans-they do prefer to shoot people with firearms:Periscopic has an excellent animated graphic showing the number of murders by gun in 2013 (11, 419) and adjacent to that number is the total years of life lost (505, 025).

So the American's (Europe is NATO and NATO is run by the USA so there is no distinct Europe) and Saudi's are whining about the practices in the Islamic Caliphate? It is ludicrous to believe that Saudi and American strategists are shocked by the Islamic Caliphate's tactics. The Americans and Saudi's were responsible for the Caliphate's creation through misguided invasions of Iraq, ham-handed regime change efforts in Syria and Egypt (USA assisted in the overthrow of Egypt's Morsi), and reckless favoritism of the Sunni over the Shia. The opportunist strategy and tactics used by Americans to destabilize Syria, and attempted in Iran (assassinations, sanctions, and cyberwar), were brazenly employed in the Ukraine. It's all of a piece with the objective of creating enough chaos on/in the borders of Russia and China so that the spillover floods and destabilizes the governments of those nation-states.

Perhaps it is not worth caring about the self-destruction of the human species. Maybe it's the nihilists, destructive capitalists, and Wahhabi's who've got it right. They always have the upper hand it seems justifying the wanton destruction of life by couching it in mystical religion backed by monetary power (or maybe it should be the other way around). The Cann

"The tortured animal subjects of neuro-scientific experiments, the suffering of the unemployed, the displaced, the impoverished are all an acceptable price for progress towards modernity, they are

unavoidable casualties in our wars for freedom, democracy and prosperity, the spiritual mimesis of which is of course the tortured Christ. Moreover our assumption that there is a linear progress in this death-march towards the modern also closes off alternative histories, so that our recollection of the past becomes merely a curiosity that allows us to marvel at our progress from those savage origins. The savages then become exemplars of not just ignorance but also illegitimate violence, violence which does not stem from Reason and a desire for Progress, but violence that is atavistic, primitive and animalistic. More widely, the project of modernity was also enabled by the possibility that war itself could become fabulously profitable and in so doing also made State-sponsored warfare a means for the Sacred Empowerment of the colonial and eventually global social order...Violence also links to the sacred as a systematic and historically evolved means for the accumulation of power and wealth through war and violence, for which the sacrifice of bodies and lives is necessary...The idea of the "war machine" references relentless and un-merciless force, constructed by civil society but always escaping its control - driven by the search for profit from even the most brutal kinds of economic and financial production."

+++++

American War Machine Ramping Up for Revenge:

U.S. Media Role is to Pacify the Nation

"The most effectual engines for pacifying a nation are the public papers... A despotic government always keeps a kind of standing army of news-writers who, without any regard to truth or to what should be like truth, invent and put into the papers whatever might serve the ministers. This suffices with the mass of the people who have no means of distinguishing the false from the true paragraphs of a newspaper." Thomas Jefferson

"Freedom of the press is another of the principal slogans of pure democracy...The capitalists have always use the term freedom to mean freedom for the rich to get richer and for the workers to starve to death. In capitalist usage freedom of the press means

freedom of the rich to bribe the press and freedom to use their wealth to shape and fabricate so-called public opinion. In this respect, too, the defenders of pure democracy prove to be defenders of an utterly foul and venal system that gives the rich control over the mass media. They prove to be deceivers of the people, who, with the aid of plausible, fine-sounding, but thoroughly false phrases, divert them from the concrete historical task of liberating the press from capitalist enslavement..." <u>V.I. Lenin</u>

According to Stars & Stripes, United States Air Force Captain William Dubois—30 years old--was killed when the F-16 he was piloting on a mission against the Islamic State crashed. Marine Lance Cpl. Sean Neal, 19, of Riverside, California died in Iraq from a noncombat related injury. Marine Cpl. Jordan Spears, 21, of Memphis, Ind., was lost at sea while conducting flight operations in the North Arabian Gulf.

Does anyone care or even notice?

These deaths were part of Operation Inherent Resolve, the American military operation designed to eliminate the Islamic Caliphate and the Syrian government run by Bashar Assad. Operation Inherent Resolve is a minor sub-plot in the grand opera/geo-strategy of the United States of America. The final act of the geopolitical opera envisioned by the grand brains of the United States is to either contain or destabilize Russia and China, and corral the lesser BRICS (Brazil, India, and South Africa.

Over the past two decades the United States and Western Europe have been burned badly by the shoddy thinking of its strategists, economists, financiers, policy makers, politicians, academicians and military leaders.

They chose to sacrifice trillions of dollars (US) in treasure and millions of lives (soldiers, civilians killed, wounded, displaced) only to lose the wars in Iraq, Afghanistan, Syria, and Libya. They have created chaos in the Middle East/Persian Gulf apparently by design.

They stood idly by while Palestinian children were slaughtered by

Israel. They clapped quietly as a military coup was undertaken in Egypt that restored the dictatorial status quo there meaning arms transfers and military cooperation could return to normal.

The Americans and West Europeans incited revolution in Ukraine and looked the other way as Nazi's brazenly assisted in the overthrow of a democratically elected government there. When Russia balked and smartly seized Crimea the Americans and Europeans were embarrassingly out maneuvered. When China allowed Edward Snowden (NSA whistleblower) to leave Hong Kong and Russia decided to allow him to stay in Russia, the Americans and Europeans were aghast at knowing they were, once again outmatched.

Further, the dunderheads in America and Western Europe finally succeeded in bringing an old Cold War nightmare to reality: their self-aggrandizing actions caused Russia and China to embrace in the form of economic and military trade deals that cut out the United States and Europe. Once again Russia has bested the Americans and Western Europeans by ditching the South Stream pipeline in favor of a pipeline to Turkey leaving Southern Europe in energy jeopardy.

Revenge!

In the cities and towns of the United States and Western Europe citizens are on edge about matters of life-security: employment, food, shelter, clothing, health insurance, education. Millions are unemployed or just culled from the statistical tables, forgotten. Children are going hungry. Immigrants are feeling the brunt of national anxiety/jingoism as they always do before street violence and war take place.

Class warfare is visible from the streets of Ferguson, Missouri to Detroit, Michigan. The classic hit song "Monster" by Steppenwolf sums it up "The cities have turned into jungles and corruption is strangling' the land. The police force is watching the people and the people just can't understand. We don't know how to mind our own business 'cause the whole world's got to be just like us. Now we are fighting a war over there, no matter who's the winner we can't pay the cost." The United States of America can't even field a high speed bullet train.

Only a global economic and kinetic war is going to satiate the hunger for revenge that the top echelons of American and Western European leadership currently display.

American President Obama will initiate the big war and President Jeb Bush will accelerate it. During the American presidential election all citizens will agree that the big war for American dominance is a given and not up for debate. The flood gates of cash will be opened by the US Congress even as social security and safety net benefits are slashed. It has all been decided in advance.

And now's the time for war. Who is going to cover the war for the masses? How will anyone really know what's going on?

Is it not genius that the media that would have provided the public with war news has been crippled through the prosecution and intimidation of journalists like James Risen, or of whistleblowers like John Kiriakou languishing in a federal prison? Then there is the collusion between the American government and media concerns like the New York Times which makes determining what is propaganda and actionable news difficult. The world knows that the US government, through the National Security Agency, is listening in: Those who might lead antiwar rebellions, or write contrarian reports, can be tracked and eliminated.

According to the Pew Research Journalism Project 25 percent of the 952 local television stations in the United States do not produce their own news products relying instead on contractors or sharing arrangements with third parties. Newsroom reductions in force continue across most mainstream media brands which--in spite of the hype over niche news outlets like Buzzfeed, Mashable, Politico, Vice News and Vox--still produce the bulk of the news products that Americans feed off of. And mainstream media continues to cut its news sectors. According to the Pew Research Journalism Project, "Full-time professional newsroom employment declined another 6.4% in 2012 with more losses expected for 2013. Gannett alone is estimated to have cut 400 newspaper jobs while the Tribune Co. announced 700 (not all of them in the newsroom).""

A clear and present danger to the reading, listening and seeing public is the growth of sponsored/biased journalism masking as news. Native Advertising is a multibillion dollar industry and growing. Nearly every news organization in the United States is in on the game in which requiring journalists/reporters write with the sponsor/advertiser in mind, not the public and national interest.

Custom Propaganda

According to the Pew Research Journalism Project "the overlap between public relations and news noted in last year's State of the News Media report became even more pronounced. One of the greatest areas of revenue experimentation now involves website content that is paid for by commercial advertisers – but often written by journalists on staff – and placed on a news publishers' page in a way that sometimes makes it indistinguishable from a news story. Following the lead of early adapters like The Atlantic and Mashable, native advertising, as it is called by the industry, caught on rapidly in 2013. The New York Times, The Washington Post and most recently The Wall Street Journal have now begun or announced plans to begin devoting staff to this kind of advertising, often as a part of a new "custom content division." eMarketer predicts that native ads spending will reach $2.85 billion by 2014.

Many of these publishers initially expressed caution over such ads, with Wall Street Journal editor-in-chief Gerard Baker even describing it as a "Faustian pact." In the end, though, many publishers eventually came down with a conclusion similar to Baker's, who said that he was "confident that our readers will appreciate what is sponsor-generated content and what is content from our global staff," according to a statement released by The Journal. That may be the case, and it could also be the case that stories created for and paid for by advertisers do not bother consumers as long as they are a good read. At this point, though, there is little if any public data that speak to consumer response one way or the other."

A similar model has long been in operation with heavyweight think tanks like the Brookings Institution who receive funding from foreign sources/sponsors to, ultimately, influence policy makers in Washington, DC. Once again the notorious non-profit NGO's reveal their true colors: "Show us the money and we'll justify anything!

Perhaps the day will come when the pundits, journalists, think tank mavens, and retired war machine veterans will be required to dress like NASCAR or Formula One race car drivers whose clothing is littered with patches advertising this and that corporation/sponsor.

Mind, Soul and Dreams Owned by Disney, Comcast, Fox, CBS, Pearson

Do you spends hours watching television until you drift into sleep? Do you read a newspaper or magazine during breakfast or lunch? Do you frequent websites that only cater to your ideology? What feeds your mind and creates your identity?

Who, really, are you? It's an important question to ask yourself.

In the original Total Recall Arnold Schwarzenegger plays a character named Quaid. He thinks that he really is Quaid, a construction worker married to a beautiful wife played by the Sharon Stone. Events transpire that reveal Quaid is really Hauser, a sinister government agent (also played by Schwarzenegger) in collusion with the oppressive Governor Cohaagen of a Mars mining colony. After a violent encounter with Cohaagen's henchmen, Quaid discovers he has killing skills he was unaware of. A rough and tumble scene with Stone follows and ends with Stone revealing to Quaid: "Your whole life is just a dream…implanted by 'the agency.'"

Later Quaid comes to find out that he really is Hauser. This revelation comes via Hauser speaking to Quaid from a prerecorded video displayed on a laptop television: "Hauser: Howdy, stranger! This is Hauser. If things have gone wrong, I'm talking to myself and you don't have a wet towel around your head. Now, whatever your name is, get ready for the big surprise. You are not you, you're me."

Here is a sampling of the vertically integrated companies that make you not you, but them: Disney owns ABC News, ESPN, Touchstone Pictures, Marvel Comics, Cruise Lines, Hyperion Books and Reedy Energy Services. Comcast owns NBC Universal, the Philadelphia Flyers, and is attempting to acquire Time Warner Cable. Fox News Corporation owns the Dow Jones & Company (Wall Street Journal, Barron's, DJX, etc.), Harper Collins Publishers, Move, Inc. (real estate news), 20th Century Fox, Fox News Channel, and Amplify (educational products for K-12). CBS owns Simon & Schuster, CNET, the Smithsonian Network, and 130 radio stations. Time Warner owns CNN, Time magazine, HBO, MAX, Sports Illustrated Kids, and People Magazine. Pearson influences the course of American education through its publishing houses, digital learning platforms, and a 50 percent interest in the Economist Magazine, Penguin Random House and the Financial Times.

Millions of 19, 21 and 30 year olds—civilians and not--are going to going to be killed, maimed, wounded and displaced in the coming years. Try to find out why.

+++++

Modern Day America: One Step Away from the Third Reich

"Unbeknownst to most Americans the United States is presently under thirty presidential declared states of emergency. They confer vast powers on the Executive Branch including the ability to financially incapacitate any person or organization in the United States, seize control of the nation's communications infrastructure, mobilize military forces, expand the permissible size of the military without congressional authorization, and extend tours of duty without consent from service personnel. Declared states of emergency may also activate Presidential Emergency Action Documents and other continuity-of-government procedures which confer powers on the President, such as the unilateral suspension of habeas corpus—that appear fundamentally opposed to the American constitutional order. Although the National Emergencies Act, by its plain language, requires the Congress to vote every six

months on whether a declared national emergency should continue, Congress has done only once in the nearly forty year history of the Act." Patrick Thronson, Michigan Journal of Law (2013, Vol 46).

A bit of irony, perhaps, that on November 4, 2014—as Americans go to the polls to cast their ballots for a slate of politicians at the local, state and federal levels—the august citizens of the United States will also celebrate the birth of the National Security Agency (NSA).

On November 4, 1952 the NSA was created by a Presidential Executive Order signed by then president Harry Truman. Earlier that year, in January 1952, Truman's state of the union address focused on the Korean War, the global Soviet-Communist threat, the "Iran oil situation", and the need to increase the production of US military equipment for use by American forces, and for transfer to Western European Allies. Truman called on Americans to seek guidance in the God of Peace even as a brutal shadow war was being waged by the United States to eliminate popularly elected "leftist" governments.

In 1953 Dwight D. Eisenhower was elected to the American presidency and with him came John Foster and Allan Dulles, two political appointees who would, it turns out, seek the counsel and expertise of "former" Nazi executioners, scientists and intelligence operatives. J Edgar Hoover, then director of the Federal Bureau of Investigation (FBI), was already on the case using whatever resources were at his disposal—including Nazis--to hunt down unionists, communists, dissenters and radicals wherever they might be. According to the UK's Guardian newspaper, Truman had this to say about Hoover and his FBI, "We want no Gestapo or secret police. FBI is tending in that direction. They are dabbling in sex-life scandals and plain blackmail… Edgar Hoover would give his right eye to take over, and all congressmen and senators are afraid of him."

From 1953-1961, Eisenhower, as Commander in Chief, constructed a nascent military-intelligence-law enforcement-industrial complex influenced directly by Nazi ideology and technological know-how. No wonder he warned the world about his creation, the military-industrial complex. At one time in the early 21st Century it was uncomfortable to call out America's ties to the Nazis. But that has changed particularly with the release of Eric Lichtblau's The Nazis Next Door (2014) and The Collaboration by Ben Urwand. It has also been confirmed by the overthrow of a nationally elected leader in Ukraine—Victor Yanukovych--and the open support of neo-Nazi groups largely responsible for that event. Is it a coincidence that the head of the CIA, John Brennan, visited with the neo-Nazi usurpers not long after the coup given the CIA's history?

Do You Want to Know a Secret, do, da, do?

According to Lichtblau, writing in the New York Times, "The full tally of Nazis-turned-spies is probably much higher', said Norman Goda, a University of Florida historian…but many records remain classified even today, making a complete count impossible. U.S. agencies directly or indirectly hired numerous ex-Nazi police officials and East European collaborators who were manifestly guilty of war crimes, he said. Information was readily available that these were compromised men. The wide use of Nazi spies grew out of a Cold War mentality shared by two titans of intelligence in the 1950s: Mr. Hoover, the longtime F.B.I. director, and Mr. Dulles, the C.I.A. director."

Over at Antiwar.com, in "Federal Agencies Just Doing Whatever They Want Now", Lucy Steigerwald comments wryly on

Lichtblau's findings. "…the CIA hid their precious assets from Nazi hunters and prosecutors trying to deport then-old men in the 1980s and even into the '90s. Most disturbing, one of Holocaust architect Adolf Eichmann's little buddies, Otto von Bolschwing, was protected until 1982, when he conveniently died of a brain disorder before he could be deported or prosecuted. Famously, Nazi rocket scientists were picked up by America to prevent their expertise from falling into Soviet hands. Maybe an exception to the prickly feeling that letting heinous war criminals off the hook is not what America was supposed to be doing when it won the good war in a heroically-sepia montage could be made for geniuses like Wernher Von Braun. Von Braun was a rocket scientist and "honorary" SS member under the Nazis, and he helped America get to the moon (which is neat, so that apparently makes his debated level of involvement/enthusiasm for the party acceptable.) What exactly did von Bolschwing contribute to America after happily joining the SS in 1933 to make ignoring his crimes worthwhile? What's the purpose of this kind of grim revelation? There are several.

One, they diminish the moral high ground about the Second World War that the US clings to desperately to this day. Yes, everyone who isn't literally Adolph Hitler gets to feel pretty good about themselves, so anyone not allied with Hitler must be doing the right thing. Yet, helping to plan the Final Solution is forgivable if the CIA really wants you around. Another more contemporary reason to be horrified by this revelation is that it is just one outrage of many. Sharing the CIA's dark corner is most of the other big-name, secretive agencies. For the past 18 months, the National Security Agency's (NSA) massive campaign of spying has been big news. Less prominent were stories that suggest the Federal Bureau of Investigation (FBI) and Drug Enforcement Administration (DEA) are also playing the part of secretive, unaccountable rulers."

Welcome to the Reich, American Style

William Binney, former NSA employee and whistleblower, stated that the NSA had gone "totalitarian". In an interview with DW he likened the NSA and the US government to the Third Reich.

Binney: "Sure, they haven't gone that far yet [as the Nazis and East German Stassi], but they tried to shut down newspaper reporters like Jim Risen…Look at the NDAA Section 1021, that gave President Obama the ability to define someone as a terrorist threat and have the military incarcerate them indefinitely without due process. That's the same as the special order 48 issued in 1933 by the Nazis, [the so-called Reichstag Fire Decree]. Read that - it says exactly the same thing. These were totalitarian processes that were instituted…Totalitarianism comes in the form first of knowledge of people and what they're doing, and then it starts to transition into using that power against people. That's what's happening - in terms of newspaper reporters, in terms of crimes. That's a direct violation of our constitution.

DW: But surely the difference is that there was an ideological regime behind the Stasi and the Nazis.

Binney: You mean like putting people like John Kiriakou in prison for exposing torture and giving the torturers immunity? That's what our country's coming to. That's what we did. That's disgraceful. The motives of totalitarian states are not exactly the same every time, but they're very similar: power, control and money…We're focusing now on everyone on the planet - that's a change from focusing on organizations that were attempting to do nasty things. When you focus on everybody, you're moving down that path towards population control."

Ingeniously Produced from Concentration Camps: Data "Comes to Light"

Many advances in warfare can be traced to Nazi innovations built on the backs of tortured souls. For example, air and ship crew survivability in frigid seas is just one of them: "…the Germans noted the terrible loss of critical personnel in sudden cold water immersion accidents. The sinking of the Bismarck and loss of airmen who bailed out alive and well into the cold North Sea during the Battle of Britain caused their physiologists and aviation medicine physicians to examine the problem. They commenced a large Research and Development program, which in part was the cause for the infamous Dachau experiments. They were the first to observe the "after drop" or continuation in reduction of body core temperature after being withdrawn from the cold water. They also experimented with survival suits and the Deutsches Textilforschunginstitut in München-Gladbach, ingeniously produced one that provided the insulation using soap bubbles which appears to have gone into limited service."

Another example is the development of the military aircraft "ejection seat". In Achtung! Schleuder-Sitzaparat by Chris Carry, German engineering was far afield of American efforts in pilot safety. "With the acquisition by the US of both German databases in egress research and actual examples of the German Heinkel explosive cartridge ejection seat immediately after the war had ended, the US began to vigorously attempt to gain greater knowledge in this overlooked area of aviation technology. The new American developmental research spurred on by acquisition of German wartime data branched off into two distinctly different approaches towards the same end, one taken by the US Air Force and one by the US Navy."

Exceptionalism and Innovative Torture Techniques Led to Technological Advances

How could human beings engage in such hideous experiments on other human beings? Well, that is a time tested formula: Indoctrinate the masses into thinking that all others besides, say, Americans, are inferior, unexceptional, demons and insects. The world is witnessing just that as the US government, its allies and its media and academic proxies seek to reduce the Russians, Arabs, Chinese, Iranians--and the immigrants, unemployed and impoverished in the United States--down to the level of parasitic microbes.

Just how does that mentality work?

For that answer we turn to the UK's Telegraph for an article written in 2008 by Richard Evans. "The answer springs from the fact that medicine was both dominant in the world of science under the Third Reich, and closely allied to the Nazi project… After all, German medical science had uncovered the causes of several major diseases and contributed massively to improving the health of the population over the previous decades. Surely, therefore, it was justified in eliminating negative influences as well? What underpinned this behavior was a widespread belief that some people were less than human, relegated to a lower plane of existence by their inherited degeneracy – or their race. For German doctors, a camp inmate was either a racially inferior subhuman, a vicious criminal, a traitor to the German cause, or more than one of the above. Such beings had no right to life or wellbeing – indeed, it was logical that they should be sacrificed in the interests of the survival and triumph of the German race, just as that race had to be strengthened by the elimination of the inferior, degenerate elements within it."

Evans goes on: "SS doctors used inmates to test treatments for injuries sustained in battle, cutting open their calves and sewing bits of glass or wood or gauze impregnated with bacteria into the wounds, sometimes even smashing the prisoners' bones with hammers to create a more realistic effect; again, the results were presented to scientific conferences without anyone offering any criticism of the methods employed. Perhaps the most enthusiastic user of human guinea pigs was the ambitious young SS doctor Sigmund Rascher, who employed camp inmates at Dachau to test the human body's reactions to rapid decompression and lack of oxygen, in an attempt to help pilots forced to parachute out of their planes at high altitudes.

He called some of his research sessions 'terminal experiments'. He measured the time it took his subjects to die as their air supply was gradually thinned out. He showed his work, which led to the deaths of between 70 and 80 prisoners, to a conference of Luftwaffe medical experts in September 1942. The following month, Rascher presented the results of another experiment to a conference of 95 medical scientists in Nuremberg. This time, he showed how long inmates dressed in Luftwaffe uniforms and life jackets could survive in cold water, simulating conditions in the North Sea. The average time that elapsed before death, he reported, was 70 minutes. None of those listening to him raised any ethical objections."

Albert Camus offers a sort of prayer for these dark times. "All I ask is that, in the midst of a murderous world, we agree to reflect on murder and to make a choice. After that, we can distinguish those who accept the consequences of being murderers themselves or the accomplices of murderers, and those who refuse to do so with all their force and being. Since this terrible dividing line does actually exist, it will be a gain if it be clearly marked. Over the expanse of five continents throughout the coming years an endless struggle is going to be pursued between violence and friendly persuasion, a struggle in which, granted, the former has a thousand times the chances of success than that of the latter. But I have always held that, if he who bases his hopes on human nature is a fool, he who gives up in the face of circumstances is a coward.

And henceforth, the only honorable course will be to stake everything on a formidable gamble: that words are more powerful than munitions."

+++++

Interview with Teheran-based FARS News Agency (FNA)

Independent American journalist says the United States has been long supporting totalitarian regimes such as the governments of Bahrain and Egypt in order to advance its destructive foreign policy goals. John Stanton, who has recently likened the conduct of the US government to the Nazi regime under Adolf Hitler, also says that the Obama administration has launched a massive campaign against the progressive media and their freedom-seeking journalists who are trying to expose the malfunction and misdeeds of the White House and Pentagon.

"President Obama's administration has pursued national security journalists and whistleblowers with a vigor never seen in American history using, on occasion, World War I era legislation to do so," said John Stanton in an interview with Fars News Agency. "If, indeed, the United States' is pushing back against challenges to its hegemony through **overt/covert** global **operations**, then it is to the advantage of American leadership to limit the visual-**text** based reporting of war by independent journalists or media outlets inclined to be anti-American, **or critical of the US government**, in their views." According to Stanton, the American people don't confide in the mechanisms and structures of the ruling establishment anymore, and this was reflected in the surprisingly low turnout at the recent mid-term Congressional elections in the United States.

John Stanton is an independent journalist specializing in national security and political matters. His writings and commentary have been cited in different publications. His articles regularly appear on the political newsletter CounterPunch co-founded by the late Alexander Cockburn and Jeffrey St. Clair. He leads a seminar on national security at a private school in the Washington, DC metro region.

The following is the text of FNA's interview with Mr. John Stanton.

Q: Many critics of President Obama accuse him of breaching the freedom of speech and press freedoms. One of the examples they cite is the US government's prosecution of the Pulitzer Prize-winning American journalist James Risen, who has made significant revelations about the complicity of the CIA in running a covert operation to disrupt and damage Iran's nuclear program in 2000. It's said that Risen's email and phone communications with the former CIA Operations Officer Jeffrey Alexander Sterling, who disclosed important information about the "Operation Merlin" to him, were illegally monitored by the federal government. What do you think about Risen's case? Don't these practices violate the principles of the US Constitution and those values which the American society is said to be oriented on?

A: The United States of America fights for its interests which are designed by its ruling plutocracy, classes. To insist that the United States fights for democracy is incorrect as it supports totalitarian governments the world over: Bahrain and Egypt are just two of many. No nation on Earth operates in any ideal way except insofar as its interests are served. In this respect the United States is no different than any other nation. The difference lies in the extraordinarily immense power that the United States has and the inability of the American people to think critically and affect change through the ballot box or a boycott of it.

It is common for American leaders to promote democracy and talk about the United States in mythic terms but most Americans do not believe any longer in this bombast. Proof of that is in the recent national elections in the United States in which only 36.3 percent of registered voters took the time to cast ballots: A figure not seen since 1942. Only seven states had participation over the 50 percent mark with some states as low as 28 percent. This data is from the United States Elections Project.

It is instructive to look at how American leaders view their own people. Consider the plight of the residents of the city of Detroit, Michigan cut off from clean water or the lockdown of Boston, Massachusetts in the hunt for one perpetrator of the Boston Marathon bombings. Consider too the national child poverty rates, the unemployed, and those simply cast aside through the manipulation of government labor figures by economists. Most Americans recognize that the stunning rise in the American stock indices have minimal relation to the daily lives of the middle to lower economic classes. In short voting is inconsequential when the two parties—Republican and Democrat—are nearly one in the same.

To analyze the United States it is imperative to view its people, culture, actions, strategies, operations and tactics through its history and instruments of national power. Its history is well known. Lesser known are its instruments of national power: diplomacy, information, military, economic, financial, law enforcement, intelligence and human capital. These instruments of power are substantial individually and, when combined, are wickedly formidable. It is abo important to not that these instruments of national power are sometime brought to bear on America's own people. In his 2010 US National Security Strategy statement, President Obama indicated that foreign and domestic strategies and operations are essentially indistinct.

Q: In one of your recent articles, you've compared the policies and actions of the US government to those of the Nazi Germany under the late dictator Adolph Hitler. Do you really see any connections between the US government in the 21st century and the Third Reich? What similarities have you

identified in their political, economic, intelligence and security approaches?

A: United States history is one of violence and that continues in the first part of the 21st Century. According to Zoltan Grossman in his History of Military Interventions since 1890, the American government has taken military action hundreds of times against its own people and other countries.

The United States of America has been engaged in a War on Terror, in various guises, for nearly two decades now. At 15 years in length, the Afghanistan occupation is the longest conflict in America's relatively young history. The Iraq occupation technically lasted for roughly 9 years though the United States always maintained a robust military and intelligence presence in Iraq after "exiting" in 2012.

In reality the United States never left Iraq -- and will not leave Afghanistan -- and has embarked on a third military occupation of that country ostensibly to fight the Islamic Caliphate. During the week of 12 November 2014, the world learned that America's plan is to eliminate the Syrian government of President Assad while simultaneously destroying the Islamic Caliphate and Al-Qaeda. The plan was the worst kept secret in Washington, DC.

Clearly, the coming military engagement pitting the United States of America against Syria and Iraq, Sunni and Shia and Kurd will require a sizable United States military force and a long term commitment of national will and treasure. Further, the interests of many nations are at stake: Saudi Arabia, Qatar, Israel, Jordan, Kuwait and Turkey are among them.

But the matter is far more significant in terms of the ongoing global geopolitical competition. The United States seeks to weaken both Russian and Chinese interests in the Middle East, Persian Gulf regions and, indeed, destabilize the internal operations of those two nations.

Q: What role do the US mainstream media play in promoting and expanding Washington's foreign policy doctrine? You

have called the mass media one of the US's powerful instruments of national power. This is while the majority of newspapers, TV channels and radio stations in the United States are said to be run independently and without government support or intervention. What's your perspective on that? Does the US government really use the media as a leverage to destabilize the "unfriendly" nations and incite violence and unrest in other parts of the world?

A: In essence the world is witnessing the 21st Century response of the United States to the challenges cutting into its global supremacy and competency: the curtain has been torn down--not just pulled back. Consider these "threats" the exposure by Edward Snowden of the extent of American espionage, the significant economic challenges posed by the BRICS and the Shanghai Cooperation Organization, the growing military might of China and Russia and the threat their bilateral relationships pose to American interests, the specter of another financial crisis, the result of quantitative easing and austerity measures and the inability to put significant portions of Americans back to work.

At some point during President Obama's presidency, the American military, industrial, corporate, financial, academic plutocracy convinced the American Commander-in-Chief that his second term was the time to push back against these challenges by using United States' instruments of national power to wage war of every type: Currency manipulation, cyberwar, sanctions, military and intelligence operations to destabilize "elected" governments-- Ukraine and Hong Kong, China for example--and disinformation operations; in short, a full-spectrum, all of government, and all of society effort to pacify the those who pose challenges to America.

And the citizens have consented to it all. Some time ago (2011) I wrote a paper titled The American National Security Consciousness, Culture and State. In that work I stated the following:

"A National Security Consciousness is firmly implanted in the psyche of the United States of America.Consequently, a National

Security Culture and State has emerged as the defining characteristic of America in the early part of the 21st Century. This development was nearly a century in the making proceeding in fits and starts from the second decade of the 20th Century until the insurgent attacks of September 11, 2001 on New York City and Arlington, Virginia. Following that event, Whole of Government, Whole of Society strategies, tactics and operations were initiated to mobilize all of America's Instruments of National Power to secure its Homeland. The American public has sanctioned this vision and mission. Behind the veil of the National Security Consciousness, Culture and State is the engine that powers the United States: American Capitalism with all its creative beauty and terrible destruction, and cyclic crises that capitalism demands.

At the helm of the mighty American National Security machine are Four Controlling Domains, one of which is Big Media (a subset of the Corporate Domain). Through Big Media, and with the other Controlling Domains' inputs, the consciousness of the American public has been shaped for acceptance of this new national security paradigm and existence within it. The American people have legitimized his reality through the electoral process [such as it is]. The process leading to the American National Security Consciousness, Culture, and State was not the result of a conspiratorial process. The transition to the national security reality was openly discussed by the Four Controlling Domains via Big Media."

It is easy to see why the media in the United States needs to be brought under some firmer form of control. James Risen's case is significant not so much for the subject matter of his reporting but that Risen is a member of the establishment. New York Times, which "plays ball" with the United States' government and military, typically holding back stories that ostensibly might compromise American national security. It appears lessons must be harsh even for a quasi-mouthpiece like te New York Times.

President Obama's administration has pursued national security journalists and whistleblowers with a vigor never seen in American history using, on occasion, World War I era legislation to do so. If, indeed, the United States is pushing back against challenges to its hegemony through global **overt/covert operations**, then it is to the advantage of American leadership to limit the visual-**text** based reporting of war by independent journalists or media outlets inclined to be anti-American, **or critical of the US government,** in their views. **Note that** the world knows that the Internet and World Wide Web are, according to United States' military doctrine, battlefields like any other. As such, the world should not be surprised that military information support operations (MISO) being waged by the Pentagon and the affiliated national security machinery will seek to manipulate everything from social media to television, radio broadcasts.

With a compliant mainstream media, and one very much reduced in size -- foreign bureaus for example -- by a loss of advertising and subscribers, there will be no clear picture of US war-making anywhere in the world. Note [that] embedded reporters are censored. The American people will be less informed than they already are. The ramifications for the electoral process are severe.

I'd like to leave you with an excerpt from Paul Virilio, one of my favorite writers. This is from his work Strategy of Deception, Verso Books (2000). I think he "called it" right a long time ago. Looking at the chaos going on in the world today, and the reduction of the nation-state, through privatization and austerity, to a security apparatus and financial guarantor, the following passage is informative.

For want of being able to abolish the bomb, we have decided then to abolish the state-- a nation state which is now charged with all sovereignist vices and all nationalist crimes thereby exonerating a military industrial complex which has spent a whole century innovating in horror and accumulating the most terrifying weapons from asphyxiating gases and bacteriological weapon,s to the thermonuclear device not to mention the future ravages of the information bomb or genetic bomb that will be capable not merely of abolishing the nation state but the people **and** the population by the genomic modification of the human race…the United States is aiming to attain the blessed state of a deterrence without an adversary or partner…Recent conflicts will merely have been arms fairs for American military equipment, new ways of promoting weapons and disastrously re-stimulating the military-industrial complex…The question which now arises is whether we have the freedom to say no to the promise of a yet more American Century that lies before us or no to the nihilistic discourse which the America of perspective and trans-appearance has been trotting out for 600 years."

Interview by Kourosh Ziabari, FNA

+++++

U.S. Treasury's Office of Terrorism and Financial Intelligence:

A Fusion Center for United Against Nuclear Iran & Foundation for Defense of Democracies?

"The Justice department would like to the see the UANI lawsuit go away as it is aware that what is being described as "law enforcement" documents would include both privileged and classified Treasury Department work product relating to individuals and companies that it has investigated for sanctions busting. Passing either intelligence related or law enforcement documents to a private organization is illegal but the Justice Department's only apparent concern is that the activity might be exposed. There is no indication that it would go after UANI for having acquired the information and it perhaps should be presumed that the source of the leak is the Treasury Department itself." Phil Giraldi

"Enforcing those AIPAC-endorsed sanctions has been the happy task of the U.S. Treasury's Office of Terrorism and Financial Intelligence. Created in early 2004 after intensive lobbying by AIPAC and its associated think tank, the Washington Institute for Near East Policy, the TFI unit has been aptly described as "a

sharp-edged tool forged principally to serve the Israel lobby."
With David S. Cohen succeeding Stuart Levey as Under Secretary
for Terrorism and Financial Intelligence in January 2011, a
leading journalist on the Middle East was later prompted to call
the position "a job which seems reserved for pro-Israeli neo-cons
to wage economic warfare against Tehran." In recent days,
Cohen's TFI unit has been eagerly waging economic warfare
against Damascus. Daniel L. Glaser, the Assistant Secretary for
Terrorist Financing, has just completed a tour of Lebanon and
Jordan to secure their compliance with economic sanctions against
the Assad government. In Beirut, the U.S. Embassy announced that
Glaser was pressing the authorities to "remain vigilant against
attempts by the Syrian regime to evade U.S. and EU sanctions."
Maidc O Cathail

So now that U.S. Attorney General Eric Holder has invoked the
U.S. States Secret privilege in the matter of Victor Restis & EST v
United Against Nuclear Iran, American citizens might come to
understand why foreign nations like China, Russia, Egypt and the
United Arab Emirates treat American non-profits or non-
governmental organizations (NGO's) with scorn. Some of these
U.S. Internal Revenue Service tax-exempt, 501C3 .org's, or
"Associations", operating overseas are nearly the equivalent of
U.S. embassies: U.S. intelligence operatives and free market
ideologues populate leadership and staff positions. Funding for
their operations are a mix of U.S. government and corporate
largess. Private donations figure as well. In some cases they are
not-so-subtle advocates for regime-change.

Robert Merry's piece April 2012 piece in The Atlantic does a fine
job of pointing out some of the more nefarious activities of NGO's
and non-profits. In *Why Do Some Foreign Countries Hate
American NGOs So Much?* Merry opines: "For anyone trying to
understand why this anger is welling up in those countries, it might

be helpful to contemplate how Americans would feel if similar organizations from China or Russia or India were to pop up in Washington, with hundreds of millions of dollars given to them by those governments, bent on influencing our politics. One supposes it would generate substantial anger among Americans if these groups tried to tilt our elections toward one party or another. But suppose they were trying to upend our very system of government, as U.S.-financed NGOs are trying to do these days in various countries--and have done in recent years in numerous locations.

Americans have a network of Israel-First organizations in the United States that are "bent on influencing our politics". They constitute a Deep State that has no remorse in sacrificing American lives and security for the benefit of Israel. Two of these non-profits are United Against Nuclear Iran (UANI) and the Foundation for the Defense of Democracies (FDD). They are part of the local, state and federal matrix of Israel-First non-profits in the U.S.

UANI has managed to get 40 American state legislatures to pass, nearly unopposed, draconian sanctions on Iran which clearly are meant to instigate the general populace to revolt. UANI claims credit for many pieces of federal legislation designed to strangle the Iranians and inflict damage of the type that sanctions leveled on the Iraqi civilian populace caused.

"UANI develops model legislation for adoption by the federal government and U.S. state governments to sever Iran from international trade and financial markets and prohibit investment in Iran. UANI's model legislation provisions were included in the federal government's Comprehensive Iran Sanctions, Accountability, and Divestment Act of 2010 (CISADA), and in debarment legislation adopted in California, Florida, New York, Indiana, Maryland and Connecticut that bars companies with Iran business from receiving taxpayer dollars."

FDD spearheads a similar program: "FDD's work has informed numerous pieces of Iran sanctions legislation, which were passed with overwhelming bipartisan congressional support, and which are now U.S. law, including the Iran Freedom and Counter-Proliferation Act of 2012 (included as part of the National Defense Authorization Act of 2013); the Iran Threat Reduction and Syria Human Rights Act of 2012; Section 1245 of the National Defense Authorization Act of 2012; and, the Comprehensive Iran Sanctions, Accountability, and Divestment Act of 2010. These laws target Iran's energy, financial, shipping, insurance, commercial, and proliferation activities, and the regime's human rights abuses. The legislative measures are widely viewed as the most robust U.S. measures yet imposed against the Iranian regime. European and Canadian officials also relied on FDD research to inform their complementary sanctions policies. Beyond gasoline, the Iran Energy Project also seeks to reduce the amount of oil revenue the Iranian regime can devote to advancing its illicit nuclear program and repressing its citizens. As part of this effort, FDD has performed studies on sanctioning Iran's Central Bank, the role of the IRGC in Iran's energy sector, and the impact of a worldwide Iranian Oil Free Zone."

According to Phillip Weiss, the US Joint Chiefs of Staff were prophetic: "In late 1947, the JCS had written that 'A decision to partition Palestine, if the decision were supported by the United States, would prejudice United States strategic interests in the Near and Middle East to the point that United States influence in the area would be curtailed to that which could be maintained by military force.' That is to say, the concern of the Joint Chiefs of Staff was not with the security of Israel-but with the security of American lives."

And so it has come to pass that the U.S. has sustained the existence of Israel through trillions (US dollars) in foreign assistance (since

1947). The U.S. has tolerated espionage and the theft of American technology, military secrets and nuclear weapons design. The U.S. government and media have been so bent by Israel-First influence that it is nearly impossible to openly criticize Israel about its thinly disguised destruction of the Palestinian people.

It just does not seem enough for the Israel-First network. How much more must Americans sacrifice for the sake of Israel? When will the big dog set things right and get the tail to begin to obey? Few Americans want to abandon Israel but to see the United States of America getting bent over the knee by Israel is unsettling.

And with the U.S. Attorney's invocation of the State Secrets privilege now providing cover for UANI's operations, it is obvious what is afoot. Circumstantially, the evidence is damning: U.S. and Israel intelligence data seems to be moving between UANI, FDD and the Office of Terrorism and Financial Intelligence in the U.S. Treasury. The three organizations form a sort of a privatized sanctions enforcement regime apparently benefiting from government intelligence operatives and/or business intelligence snoops. Where you find David S. Cohen of the Office of Terrorism and Financial Intelligence you will also find some link to UANI or FDD. And then there is the fear factor: Financial sanctions, loss of business in Israel, and loss of political office in the U.S. How two non-profits became so powerful and feared is a testimony to the strength of the Israel-First organizations and their ability to bend the political consciousness of the United States of America.

Some Items for "You" to Explore

"From: Bart Mongoven
To: Reva Bhalla
Sent: Wednesday, April 21, 2010 2:49:34 PM GMT -06:00
US/Canada Central

Our mission (in the short term) is to determine how much flexibility is in the seemingly inflexible demand that the client…Client is Honeywell, which makes surveillance equipment Iran uses to monitor/secure pipelines and (allegedly) nuclear reactors…get out of Iran "right now." The client says that it will not sign another contract but that it does not want to breach contracts that are in place. This is the position that Ingersoll Rand and Siemens have taken, and it seemed OK with UANI. At the same time, UANI is telling our client that the same pledge isn't good enough. Is UANI still in talks or putting similar pressure on those who have pledged that they will leave when current contracts are up?…How did they decide to start targeting corporations -- is there a model it is following (like the Save Darfur coalition or something else)? How do they choose their small list of targets since there are so many companies operating in Iran? Do they know people at the corporations they target? How closely do UANI and FDD work? Are there any deadlines in Iran -- elections, feared nuke tests, coming deaths of really sick clerics, etc., that requires FDD and UANI show progress quickly?"

"As for the Marc Rich case, former federal prosecutor Andrew McCarthy accurately described it as "one of the most disgraceful chapters in the history of the Justice Department." Congressional investigators called it "unconscionable." Fugitive commodities trader Marc Rich, on the run for evading nearly $50 million in taxes, found the best lawyer he could buy: former Democratic White House counsel and intimate friend of *Eric Holder*, Jack Quinn. Despite his denials, memos showed Holder knew of the pardon in advance, failed to notify prosecutors and the FBI that it was coming, "and even gave Quinn public-relations advice on getting out the 'legal merits of the case.'" The evidence clearly shows Holder and Quinn violated department protocols and colluded to keep the Justice Department out of the pardon deal.'

"The central issue in this case involves an allegation that the defendants, as senior officers, managers, agents and nominees for the **Bank of Credit and Commerce International ("BCCI"1)**, illegally and secretly sought to acquire ownership and maintain control of First American Corporation: FIRST AMERICAN CORP., et al., Plaintiffs, v. Sheikh Zayed Bin Sultan AL-NAHYAN, et al., Defendants....United States District Court, District of Columbia. November 26, 1996. William Horace Jeffress, Jr., Herbert John Miller, Jr., Douglas Frank Curtis, Martin David Minsker, **David S. Cohen, Miller, Cassidy, Larroca & Lewin, L.L.P.**, Washington, DC, William B. Shields, Washington, DC, for defendants Clark M. Clifford, Robert Alan Altman."

"David S. Cohen...Treasury undersecretary for terrorism and financial intelligence, who oversees the OFAC sanctions effort, reportedly following meetings with Israeli officials, said last week's actions were meant to "tighten the screws and intensify the economic pressure against the Iranian regime. "The US is counting on the Iranian people to turn against and overthrow their government because of sanctions-induced hardships...In reality, the sanctions target the civilian population and the "Iranian regime" won't be much affected... Despite the public relations language that "food and medicine are exempted from the brutal US-led sanctions, as OFAC well knows, the reality is something else. They know well the chilling effects of the sanctions on international suppliers of medicines and food stuffs with respect to a targeted country. The US Treasury department has thousands of gigabytes of data confirming that the boards of directors of international business do not, and will not allow their companies to risk millions of dollars in profits by technically violating any of the thousands of details in the sanctions -- many of which are subject to interpretation -- for the sake of doing business with Iran or

Syria."

"More about Stuart Levey's intimate connections to both the US Treasury and the Justice Department: After leaving the Treasury Department, Mr. Levey was a Senior Fellow for National Security and Financial Integrity at the Council on Foreign Relations. Prior to his Treasury appointment, Mr. Levey served as the Principal Associate Deputy Attorney General at the US Department of Justice, having previously served as an Associate Deputy Attorney General and as the Chief of Staff of the Deputy Attorney General. Where is Stuart Levey today? Why, he's on the HSBC Board of Directors as the Chief Legal Officer of HSBC Holdings plc, the parent company of HSBC operations worldwide. We got all this information about Mr. Levey from his HSBC bio page. There we learned that he has been the drug money-laundering megabank's Chief Legal Officer since January 2012. Thus, he would have been intimately involved in (and legally responsible for) the crafting of HSBC's December 2012 Get Out of Jail Free settlement with the Justice Department. Intelligence from **David S. Cohen's group at Treasury must have also played a role in advising Justice on the historic settlement.**"

David S. Cohen, Office of Terrorism and Financial Intelligence: "Increasing Iran's Isolation…First, we will continue to identify ways to isolate Iran from the international financial system. **We will do so by maintaining our aggressive campaign of applying sanctions against individuals and entities engaged in, or supporting, illicit Iranian activities and by engaging with the private sector and foreign governments to amplify the impact of these measures.** As part of this effort we will also target Iran's attempts to evade international sanctions through the use of non-bank financial institutions, such as exchange houses and money services businesses. And we will explore new measures to expand our ability to target Iran's remaining links to the global financial sector. In particular, we are looking carefully at actions that could increase pressure on the value of the rial. In that connection, we will continue to actively investigate any sale of gold to the Government of Iran, which can be used to prop up its currency and to compensate for the difficulty it faces in accessing its foreign reserves. We currently have authority under E.O. 13622 to target those who provide gold to the Iranian government and, as of July I, IFCA will expand that authority to target for sanctions the sale of gold to or from anyone in Iran for any purpose."

+++++

Political Duopoly in Washington Encouraging Ongoing Killing

From Missouri to Ukraine

"...in what manner does tyranny arise? --that it has a democratic origin is evident...But when [the tyrant] has disposed of foreign enemies by conquest or treaty, and there is nothing to fear from them, then he is always stirring up some war or other, in order that the people may require a leader...Has he not also another object, which is that they may be impoverished by payment of taxes, and thus compelled to devote themselves to their daily wants and therefore less likely to conspire against him?: Clearly....And if any of them are suspected by him of having notions of freedom, and of resistance to his authority, he will have a good pretext for destroying them by placing them at the mercy of the enemy; and for all these reasons the tyrant must be always getting up a war."
Plato, Book VIII

There is a lot of gnashing of teeth in the USA over the events taking place in Ferguson, Missouri, sparked by the shooting death of teenager Michael Brown. There is something for every interest group in this tragic event: race relations (and history); media manipulation; militarization of American civilian law enforcement by the Pentagon, US Congress and Israel; class warfare; globalization, income disparity; systemic political failure; Democratic and Republican Party hustler-ism; and so on. To be sure 100 PhD theses will be written using Ferguson as a topic, and Pulitzer Prizes will be awarded for journalists pushed around by the Ferguson police.

Then, in time, the whole matter will largely be forgotten by Americans as they move onto death and destruction in Ukraine, Gaza, South Sudan, Syria, Iraq, Detroit (Michigan), Chicago (Illinois), South China Sea, etc., etc., etc. Inevitably the Ferguson story will be the subject of, at least, a television movie, books, spoken-word music and verse. Heroes and scoundrels will be called out; the parade of individuals representing organizations who claim "I was at the front lines in Ferguson" will show up on talk shows across America and the world. Millions of dollars will be made by mainstream media outlets and the families involved. Congressional hearings will be held and legislation will be passed by the US Congress limiting funding for law enforcement's purchase of certain classes of military grade combat gear. Membership in pro-white and black organizations will increase. Gun sales will spike.

It will all pass before the numb eyes and brains of Americans via a television or computer screen or on the paper pages of the Sunday editions of major newspapers on the Eastern/Western American seaboards. And then the great forgetting will take place, save for the trivial reminder on the first, second, third anniversary dates during which "Remember Michael Brown" moments-of-silence will occur. It is the same formula that took place for the Boston Marathon Bombing; the Sandy Hook Elementary School shootings; the attacks of September 11, 2001; and commemorations to the dead and wounded of the wars in Iraq and Afghanistan.

Ferguson is to Obama as George W. Bush is to New Orleans

The political duopoly in America thrives on these horrific events. After all, they created the environment unfurling in Ferguson and likely to occur elsewhere in the USA. It is this political duopoly that has nearly squeezed Americans dry through socioeconomic policies designed to bankrupt and marginalize middle to lower classes of all races. The political duopoly would not exist were in not for those who support, and enforce, the two-party control of the executive, legislative and judicial branches of the American government: corporations (includes media and defense), US military services, academia, think tanks, interest groups (nonprofits), and foreign countries, companies and their agents.

The entire lot of them are indifferent to the fact that 13.4 percent of the American population (Black) makes up the majority of America's prison population or that their economic woes are equal to, or worse than, the many millions of Americans of all stripes who have no prospects of life-security (food, water, clothing, shelter, safety, work). President Barak Obama claims to be "a black man" even though he is equally "a white man". Which one are we to believe?

Obama, like all presidents before him, is responsible for setting the tone on social, economic and national security policy in the USA. But as Ferguson exploded, Obama was playing golf on Martha's Vineyard and continued to do so until the governor of Missouri, Jay Nixon (Democrat) activated that state's militia, the US National Guard.

In Obama Americans are experiencing, and the world is seeing, what future presidents of the USA will be like: largely a spectator of the US political, economic and national security machinery (except for using constitutional executive powers on behalf of those interests); purveyor of American myth and propaganda; culturally "cool" for the masses; and master of ceremonies like the State of the Union. The 21st Century president will follow Plato's path from democratic man to tyrant. Obama, and those presidents who come after, is akin to the "Nowhere Man" described in the Beatles song of the same name. But it is Plato's drum that democratic citizen, tyrant or not, marches to.

"...he lives from day to day indulging the appetite of the hour; and sometimes he is lapped in drink and strains of the flute; then he becomes a water-drinker, and tries to get thin; then he takes a turn at gymnastics; sometimes idling and neglecting everything, then once more living the life of a philosopher; often he-is busy with politics, and starts to his feet and says and does whatever comes into his head; and, if he is emulous of any one who is a warrior, off he is in that direction, or of men of business, once more in that. His life has neither law nor order; and this distracted existence he terms joy and bliss and freedom; and so he goes on...he is all liberty and equality....his life is motley and manifold and an epitome of the lives of many; --he answers to the State which we described as fair and spangled. And many a man and many a woman will take him for their pattern, and many a constitution and many an example of manners is contained in him."

We Fight Them Over There So We Can Fight American Citizens Here

So America has its lovable war-tyrant-democratic man named Obama--"a bit like you and me.". But it does not matter whether a Democrat or Republican tyrant is at the helm as the Oval Office can be counted on to represent the interests of the mighty who buttress the political duopoly. And they will go to any length to achieve their Kingdom on Earth whether it's pounding protestors in Ferguson, Missouri or instigating the shoot-down of a civilian aircraft over Ukraine. They will lie, cheat and steal from the poor and give to the rich. They twist the US Constitution and Bill of Rights to suit their needs. American citizens get no special preference from the political duopoly: citizens are petty and in the way, just like any other threat from outside US borders.

The relentless American campaign against Russia and the separatist rebels in Ukraine, and US support for military operations in Gaza, Syria, Iraq, Yemen and South Sudan, for example, is overseen by the same political duopoly that governs the US homeland.

Take a look at Urban Shield 2014, for example, that tests the mettle of SWAT, EOD and Firefighters in a competition in California. US agencies and public/private partners listed as supporting Urban Shield 2014 include the FBI, DEA, DHS, FEMA, US Army, US Marine Corps, US Navy, Lockheed Martin, and International Armored Group. One of Urban Shield's most notable sponsors is EXELIS. Its Board of Directors includes former undersecretary of defense John Hamre (Center for Strategic and International Studies in Washington, DC) and former US Army general Paul Kern (The Cohen Group). The CEO and President of EXELIS David Melcher, is a former US military lieutenant general and a Board of Trustee member at the National Defense Industrial Association. EXELIS has a broad array of capabilities with airborne remote sensing, command and control, and surveillance and reconnaissance among them. Its customers, naturally, are all the US military branches and the US Department of Homeland Security.

According to Forbes Magazine "a new wave of such military-to-commercial innovations is beginning to reach the marketplace as overseas wars wind down. The best known are drones originally developed to find fleeting threats, but the big opportunity for entrepreneurs may lie not so much in the aircraft as in the compact, high-resolution sensors that they carry. A case in point is CorvusEye 1500, a wide-area surveillance system developed by the geospatial technology unit of defense contractor Exelis (XLS). Corvus is the genus of birds to which crows and ravens belong, and CorvusEye 1500 was conceived to offer domestic law-enforcement agencies the kind detailed, birds-eye view of events on the ground that previously was available only to warfighters."

Washington Encouraging Ongoing Killing: Streets of Ferguson or Donetsk, No Matter

Karel Van Wolferen's *The Ukraine, Corrupted Journalism and the Atlanticist Faith* sums up the handiwork of America's political duopoly as practiced outside its borders.

"America's history, since the demise of the Soviet Union, of truly breathtaking lies: on Panama, Afghanistan, Iraq, Syria, Venezuela, Libya and North Korea; its record of overthrown governments; its black-op and false flag operations; and its stealthily garrisoning of the planet with some thousand military bases, is conveniently left out of consideration...It is unlikely that the American NGOs, which by official admission spent 5 billion dollars in political destabilization efforts prior to the February putsch in Kiev, have suddenly disappeared from the Ukraine, or that America's military advisors and specialized troops have sat idly by as Kiev's military and militias mapped their civil war strategy; after all, the new thugs are as a regime on financial life-support provided by Washington, the European Union and IMF. What we know is that Washington is encouraging the ongoing killing in the civil war it helped trigger...In much of the European Union the general understanding of global reality since the horrible fate of the people

on board the Malaysian Airliner [MH17] comes from mainstream newspapers and TV which have copied the approach of Anglo-American mainstream media, and have presented 'news' in which insinuation and vilification substitute for proper reporting... Nothing that I have seen or read even intimated that the Ukraine crisis – which led to coup and civil war – was created by neoconservatives and a few R2P ("Responsibility to Protect") fanatics in the State Department and the White House, apparently given a free hand by President Obama."

Obviously, Plato was way ahead of his time in figuring out what follows democracy—tyranny and war. Plato also knew that no matter the form of governance—tyranny, democracy, oligarchy/duopoly, or plutonomy—slaves were a desirable necessity for those that ruled. *"...nature herself intimates that it is just for the better to have more than the worse, the more powerful than the weaker; and in many ways she shows, among men as well as among animals, and indeed among whole cities and races, that justice consists in the superior ruling over and having more than the inferior."*

The citizens of Ferguson, Missouri know the score and they are not lone.

+++++

America's Deep State: Foreign Agents, Lobbyists, Corporations, Military-Intel

"In the period between the end of World War Two and Marshall's meeting with Truman [May 12, 1948], the Joint Chiefs of Staff had issued no less than sixteen (by my count) papers on the Palestine issue. The most important of these was issued on March 31, 1948 and entitled "Force Requirements for Palestine." In that paper, the JCS predicted that "the Zionist strategy will seek to involve [the

United States] in a continuously widening and deepening series of operations intended to secure maximum Jewish objectives." The JCS speculated that these objectives included: initial Jewish sovereignty over a portion of Palestine, acceptance by the great powers of the right to unlimited immigration, the extension of Jewish sovereignty over all of Palestine and the expansion of "Eretz Israel" into Transjordan and into portions of Lebanon and Syria. This was not the only time the JCS expressed this worry. In late 1947, the JCS had written that "A decision to partition Palestine, if the decision were supported by the United States, would prejudice United States strategic interests in the Near and Middle East" to the point that "United States influence in the area would be curtailed to that which could be maintained by military force." **That is to say, the concern of the Joint Chiefs of Staff was not with the security of Israel- but with the security of American lives."** Philip Weiss

On July 31, 2014 Wikipedia patrolman PlotSpoiler substantially altered this writer's minor Wikipedia entry placing tags questioning the legitimacy of the profile's presence on Wikipedia, and removing a number of entries.

No problem there. Wiki's guidelines supported many of the edits made to the entry.

When Steve Martin's character Navin, in the movie the Jerk, discovers that his name had been listed in a telephone book, he gets excited. In like fashion, I was pleased like Navin--some time back--when I saw my Wiki entry. Now an afterthought I rarely look at it.

But after the latest piece appeared online at Pravda (United Against Nuclear Iran Donors Identified), I was curious. Are there really pro-Israel types who spend their days on the World Wide Web looking for detractors or critics? Given Israel's current military operation, Israel's information warriors had to have carefully constructed their military information support operations (MISO) knowing that they would be hammered in the media. On that score they have performed marvelously: Pushing the success of the Iron Dome which does, in fact, not work as promoted, and focusing on tunnel destruction as the core objective when it is not.

At any rate the Wiki profile had not been substantially modified since August of 2013. Within a day or so of the previous version of this article PlotSpoiler appeared and revised the Wiki profile. Wikipedia maintains extraordinary records of revisions located under the "view history" tab. The "talk" tab sometimes leads to remarkable debates over verbiage and meanings.

So all of this would be unremarkable except for the fact that Plot Spoiler's track record indicates that he trolls Wiki to find and edit/annul, any bias or the appearance of legitimate criticism of Israel and the history and personalities that have led Israel to where it is today: Engaged in a military campaign to drive the Palestinians in Gaza into the sea.

It's Foggy

Conscious Americans should do themselves a favor and watch The Fog of War: Eleven Lessons from the life of Robert S. McNamara (Erol Morris). Commit those lessons to memory and get out on the World Wide Web and do some digging. That task is vitally important as America's leaders are taking the nation into wars that can't be won: Not against Russia, China or Iran. At home American citizens are denied access to water (Detroit) and infrastructure is in disrepair (Los Angeles). The US Constitution is broken as the CIA (executive branch) covers up torture and murder ("we tortured some folks" said President Obama) by blackmailing members of the US Senate (legislative branch). The US Supreme Court has given the American electoral process to the wealthy and corporations via its Citizens United decision.

And what can be said about the US support for the slaughter in Gaza. It's disgusting on so many levels, not the least of which is the fear that US politicians, musicians, artists, publishers, reporters and editors have of the pro-Israeli lobby here in the USA. Moreover, US military commanders like General Martin Dempsy seem to be gleeful about the prospects of waging total war against Russia just as they are about supporting Israel's destruction of Gaza.

Americans do not have a government by and for "the American people."

Foreign Power Operating in the USA: Jewish Federation, United Fund

"We have since worked with a broad coalition of Jewish and non-Jewish groups as well as with United Against Nuclear Iran (UANI) to support legislative and regulatory actions requiring divestment from companies that do business with Iran, as well other sanctions. 'Florida has been a leader in adopting strong measures to isolate the Iranian regime in the areas of procurement, divestment and banking. We encourage local communities across the U.S to join Florida to pass similar measures" said Tara Laxer, Florida Director of United Against a Nuclear Iran.' *Greater Miami Jewish Federation*

The Jewish Federation and the Jewish United Fund are two of the donors to UANI. These nonprofit organizations are part of the wider US-based, pro-Israel juggernaut that shapes American national security strategy for Israel. Through connections, money, position and power they seek to immunize Israel from criticism for its mendacious, militaristic policies. They have succeeded in marginalizing discussion of America's dangerously pro-Israel policies to the extent that the subject is taboo: Criticize Israel and automatically receive the badge of anti-Semitism. Meanwhile US warfighters have an additional cross to bear in the world of Islam as they are seen as pawns of Israel. More's the pity American foes are energized by America's blind support of a tiny nation, strategically insignificant but with a stranglehold over American national security interests.

Matt Apuzzo writing for the New York Times recently reported that the US Department of Justice has asked that United Against a Nuclear Iran's donor lists and dollar amounts not be turned over in litigation involving a defamation lawsuit. "The Justice Department has temporarily blocked the group from having to reveal its donor list and other internal documents in a defamation lawsuit filed by a Greek shipping magnate the group accused of doing business with Iran. Government lawyers said they had a "good faith basis to believe that certain information" would jeopardize law enforcement investigations, reveal investigative techniques or identify confidential sources if released."

Alex Kane of Mondoweiss wrote a piece titled "'New York Times' profile of group bent on sanctioning Iran fails to mention Israel connections," back in June 2013. With a bit of effort he was able to find a number of UNAI's contributors.

Many of UNAI's donors can easily be found by doing some research on the World Wide Web. And what one finds, of course, is a superbly networked Jewish community, most on message advocating for the interests of the Israeli government. These pro-Israel nonprofits serve as the eyes and ears for Israel in the USA and as fundraisers/donors for groups like UNAI, who themselves take guidance from the Israeli government.

80

Jewish Agency for Israel, Jewish United Fund of Israel

Americans know about the American Israel Political Action Committee and the influence they can bring to bear on American politicians and, through JINSA, American military commanders.

But fewer know about organizations like the Jewish Agency for Israel. Its annual report lists the 156 groups that make up the Jewish Federations of North America. They are located in nearly every major city in the USA.

The Jewish Agency for Israel had $478 million in revenue for 2013, according to its annual report. In that reports trends section it indicates that the Jewish Agency will work with the government of Israeli to enhance the identity of young Jews around the world. Its donor list must be the envy of every nonprofit in America. The list includes the Tisch Foundation (movies), IKEA (furniture), Rothschild Foundation (banking), Charles E. Smith (construction in Washington, DC), Larry Ellison (Oracle), John Hagee (Christian evangelical), and Siemens (telecommunications).

UANI received $25,000 in funding from the Jewish United Fund of Chicago (JUF), a powerhouse fundraising organization connecting those of the Jewish community in Chicago. According to the organization's board meeting minutes from early 2013 (readily available online), JUF has revenues of $206 million dollars. Of interest in those meeting minutes is a quote by Colonel Danny Tirza, the designer of the Security Fence that splits Israelis and Palestinians: "Not a single Palestinian home was damaged by the process [of building the fence]."

JUF allocated $30 million for Israel and Overseas Operations according to the board minutes.

JUF was one of the founders of the Israeli Action Network—along with the Jewish Council for Public Affairs and Jewish Federations of North America--whose mission is to fight against the boycott, divestiture and sanctions movement in the United States. JUF indicated in its board meeting minutes that although the American Studies Association (ASA) passed a resolution in 2013 in favor of boycotting Israeli academic institutions, the Israeli Action Network made a number of non-Jewish contacts and were able to convince a number of American university presidents to condemn the ASA resolution. The ASA described the outcome of the vote for the resolution thus: "The members of the American Studies Association have endorsed the Association's participation in a boycott of Israeli academic institutions. In an election that attracted 1252 voters, the largest number of participants in the organization's history, 66.05% of voters endorsed the resolution, while 30.5% of voters voted no and 3.43% abstained. The election was a response to the ASA National Council's announcement on December 4 that it supported the academic boycott and, in an unprecedented action to ensure a democratic process, asked its membership for their approval."

What's UANI got that Obama's justice department does not want released?

Ask the FBI and other American counterintelligence agencies two questions: How deep have Israeli operatives penetrated into America's critical infrastructure sectors, American intelligence agencies, and the US military? Who are the members of the American Deep State?

As MC Hammer once said, "Can't touch this."

+++++

The Obama Doctrine: Up Yours!

The Howard P. "Buck" McKeon National Defense Authorization Act for FY 2015 (Defense Authorization Act) should be renamed the *Howard P. "Buck" McKeon Global Manifest Destiny Act of FY2015*. The Defense Authorization Act reads like something that the Biffer-Baum Birds in *Dr. Seuss' Sleep Book* might have written. And the image that most accurately depicts the collective efforts of President Obama, the Pentagon and the US Congress in the design of American national security strategy is Dr. Seuss' illustration of the Biffer-Baum Birds constructing their nest out of bricks and threads: a precarious construction indeed.

The Defense Authorization Act, and the President's recent speech to West Point Cadets, provides unshakeable evidence that the political-military-corporate leadership learned no lessons from one unnecessarily prolonged war (Afghanistan) and one needless conflict (Iraq). The millions displaced in Iraq and Afghanistan spilling into neighboring countries like Lebanon and Pakistan; the thousands of Americans and civilians killed, wounded or collateralized (with families left adrift); the creation of failed states in Syria and Libya, and the scam that is the "promise to American combat veterans" to take care of them upon return to an increasingly dilapidated homeland are all mere lint to be brushed off the shoulders of America's elite.

Schemers

In the midst of horrific treatment of former US military personnel at the hands of the Veterans Administration and assorted military programs--and the fact that America's political and military leaders never prepared its warfighters or its citizens for over a decade of war in Iraq, Afghanistan and "on terror"—this statement from the US Congress is totally hollow. "The committee remains committed to providing America's warfighters, veterans, and their families with the care and support they need, deserve, and have earned. This bill would authorize an extension of a wide array of bonuses, special and incentive pays for the Nation's men and women in uniform."

Heath Ledger's Joker in the Dark Knight was right about "authority." Buck McKeon and his ilk "are all schemers."

The President and his handlers seek to do it all over again this time against Russia and China through the Asia Pivot. There is some sort of weird neoconservative, neoliberal monster that now seems to exist in the form of President Obama (who is this guy, really?). And that means it's "in your face" foreign and domestic policy. American activity in Ukraine serves as the best example of this "up yours" Obama Doctrine.

Up Yours! = Obama Doctrine

The Obama Doctrine narrative goes something like this: "Yeah, so we are going to brazenly assist in the overthrow of Ukraine's elected-though controversial president--with help from Brown Shirt fascist groups and the CIA and assorted NGO's. Our senior US State Department officials and senators are going to openly serve tea and crumpets to coup supporters in Maiden Square in Kiev. Once we have succeeded in toppling the elected government (nullifying the prior votes in Eastern Ukraine) we will then rob you of your Black Sea port of naval operations. Next we are going to send our vice president and CIA director to provide legitimacy to our marionettes in Kiev. After that we are going to have US military advisors/contractors assist in designing operations to destroy insurgent uprisings in Eastern Ukraine that oppose Kiev's will.

As this US government backed coup is a military operation, military information support operations (MISO) will be required and that means shaping opinion in the USA and Ukraine and the EU, which, in turn means propaganda to legitimize the coup. Yeah, you will try to get your propaganda out but it will not matter. Anyway we will trot out the Hitler ghosts for our purposes and will we get our legacy media outlets like the Washington Post and New

York Times to vilify Russia (China too). And do you know what? There is nothing you can do about it. Oh, and for good measure we are going to ensure that member of the world's richest club ascends to the presidency of the new Ukraine amidst a rigged election. And we are going to do the same thing in other countries. Up yours, man."

Forget tribal, realist, idealist, neoconservative and neoliberal theories of international relations. The world is in the midst of some sort of emergent Gang Theory of international relations in which there is no Concert of Nations, or United Nations, but a Gang of Cultures. The USA's culture of violence has made it ideally suited for such a world.

Coup's for All!

The USA has given the green light to the coups in Ukraine, Thailand and Egypt. In doing so it has remained historically consistent in its debasement of representative democracy, hiding the real agenda. There was a time when the US government, in collaboration with the mainstream media, could control the flow of information about such coups comparing them to the glorious American Revolution. The Internet and World Wide Web has changed the dynamic. America's leaders have exhausted their supply of credibility. The world has learned from Assange/Wikileaks; Edward Snowden/Glenn Greenwald; and NSA/CIA whistleblowers like John Kiriakou that the grand brains running America into the ground do so for money, power and market-share--nothing more. The ruthlessness of their buy-sell ideology is plain sight.

For example, note the similarity of the mercenary verbiage of Reuters and the Defense Authorization Act's authors in the US Congress. The 21st Century version of Idi Amin, General Abdel Fattah al-Sisi of Egypt, grabbed the presidency there recently. Al-

Sisi led the military coup that toppled the former president of Egypt, Mohamed Morsi. The turnout for Morsi was 52 percent, for al-Sisi 46 percent.

Reuters: *"One of Sisi's biggest tests will be the politically-sensitive issue of energy subsidies which drain billions of dollars from the state budget every year. Businessmen have urged Sisi to raise energy prices even though that may trigger protests, or risk sinking the economy. Investors want Sisi to end energy subsidies, impose a clear tax regime and give guidance on the direction of the exchange rate."*

US Congress Defense Authorization Act: *"This bill would also recognize the President's determination that the Arab Republic of Egypt is progressing in its democratic transition and supports the President's decision to deliver 10 Apache helicopters to Egypt for counterterrorism operations."*

In short, pillage Egypt's middle and lower classes and use the money extracted from them to bow before investors and buy weapons ostensibly for counterterrorism. In fact, when the riots over rising food and energy prices take place in Egypt, or Ukraine or Thailand, those US Apache helicopters—and other American made military/law enforcement equipment-- will be used to drive women, children and other protestors from the streets.

Will the day arrive in the USA when local and state law enforcement is absorbed completely by the Department of Defense and the Department of Homeland Security? Will officers of the National Police Department have licenses to kill?

Perhaps Ukraine is a window to the future of the USA's Republic—maybe even Thailand or Egypt.

Secret Weapon for Asia Pivot: Diplomatic Functions to the US Military

How did the Human Terrain System (HTS) emerge as one of Obama's secret weapons for the Asia Pivot? Apparently Secretary of the Army John McHugh is a proponent of the program. According to the Defense Authorization Act, PACOM gets the privilege of a Pilot Program for the Human Terrain System. "This section would require the Secretary of the Army to conduct a pilot program to utilize Human Terrain System assets in the U.S. Pacific Command area of responsibility to support Phase 0 shaping operations and to support the theater security cooperation plans of the geographic combatant commander."

Phase Zero Shaping, according to the Center for Global Development, can be seen as part of the Pentagon's absorption of US diplomatic functions normally undertaken by the US State Department. The resources and latitude that the Pentagon provides to its Geographic Combatant Commanders is very broad. "The danger in this scheme is that it puts the Pentagon in the driver's seat and threatens to militarize U.S. engagement... Interagency coordination is one thing, but assigning leadership for this integration to the Pentagon is a risky proposition... What the Pentagon is calling 'Phase Zero' sounds suspiciously like what some of us still quaintly refer to as 'diplomacy' and 'development assistance.' Given the Pentagon's massive resources compared to civilian agencies, any 'shaping' activities that emerge...are likely to reflect U.S. military priorities and give short shrift to broader political and developmental considerations. After all, DOD's primary concern in weak and failing states is to build the capacity of local security forces. Whether those forces are under effective and accountable civilian control is a secondary concern," said the Center for Global Development.

The ultimate "Up Yours" just might be saddling PACOM with the US Army's HTS.

At any rate, the Defense Authorization Act--buttressed by

Obama's recent West Point speech--has put the world on notice that "The Yanks are coming for your markets and your land!" That, of course, means more coups and, with the US national fear factor dropping, perhaps a false flag operation or two.

Starship Troopers: Kill the Bug!

The movie Starship Troopers depicts galactic traveling insects fighting against humans for domination of the vast void of space. But one need not go to the movies to understand what a clear and present danger bugs or "invasive species" are to the US Homeland and the US military. The Defense Authorization Act recognizes this. "The committee notes that in the fall of 2013, the coconut rhinoceros beetle, an invasive species to the Hawaiian Islands and Guam, was discovered on the island of Oahu and has been found on Guam since 2007. While it is unknown how the species came to Hawaii or Guam, the committee is aware that a coconut rhinoceros beetle population was identified on Joint Base Pearl Harbor-Hickam, which is in close proximity to Honolulu International Airport. Since discovering the existence of this invasive species on Hawaii, the committee notes that the Department of Agriculture has been leading the effort, jointly with the Department of Defense and appropriate State agencies, to eliminate breeding sites, and monitor and control the spread of the coconut rhinoceros beetle on the island of Oahu."

According to the US Navy's Shipboard Pest Management Manual, the German cockroach is the most common insect on US Navy surface vessels and submarines. They infest kitchen areas and lurk in the dark negatively impacting the morale of the sailors. There are scores of insects, like the Dermestid Beetle, that make their homes on US Navy vessels. Just a subtle reminder from the Earth that the most advanced American technology/weaponry literally has bugs living and breeding in and on it.

So what's the point with "invasive species"? Post-911 hysteria led to a paper in the US Army magazine Parameters discussing the use of insects by terrorists to disrupt/damage daily life in the USA. In that paper (Invasive Threats to the American Homeland by Robert Pratt), prefaced by a quote from President George W. Bush, we learn that "A 1999 study by Cornell University estimated that approximately 50,000 foreign species have invaded the United States since the 1700s, and the number in the last 30 years has increased at an alarming rate."

It is one thing to invest and engage in "pest management" but a war on terrorists and their bugs?"

Such is the warped mentality of American culture reflected in the authors of the Defense Authorization Act and, sadly, President Obama.

+++++

War Pigs Need the Draft: More Bodies, Plus Women, Necessary

"...Evil minds that plot destruction. Sorcerers of death's destruction. In the keeps turning. In the fields the bodies burning as the war machine keeps turning...Politicians hide themselves away. They only started the war. Why should they go out to fight? They leave that role to the poor." *Black Sabbath,War Pigs*

Oh, it's out there. It is the US government's Selective Service/Draft program that currently requires all males 18 years of age to willingly sign up for the opportunity to have the US government force them, under penalty of law, to work for the government in a killing and maiming capacity (military employment), or in a supporting role for those who are on the front lines doing the US government's dirty work in far away lands and, who knows, perhaps here in the USA.

The Selective Service/Draft system us in sort of a state of suspended animation to be used only when a national crisis forces the US government to dig into the pool of bodies when the volunteer military force can't handle the load placed on them by the requirements of its own government or the enemy. Open conflict with Russia, China or an intervention to stabilize a collapsed Mexican government/economy would likely necessitate activation of the Selective Service/Draft.apparatus. Already the US national security machinery is stretched to the breaking point with active duty and national guard personnel seeing multiple rotations to conflict zones on every continent. Domestically, the support network—including communities, families, volunteer organizations--for returning military personnel suffering from debilitating injuries to mind and body is nearly broken ,aided and abetted by greedy private contractors looking to make money not alleviate the suffering of the veterans.

Politicians and military commanders fear the activation of the Selective Service/Draft lottery as they would lose the ability to respond to the disgruntled or abused soldier, " You are the one who volunteered." This even though study after study shows the much ballyhooed volunteer military force exists largely because the civilian marketplace has no need for low-level labor (as it continues to jettison labor, Target for example) or the military marketing campaign that pushes the myth that military service trumps that of civilian law enforcement and first res ponders who keep American communities as :"free and safe" as possible.

According to Mint Press, '"The military also seems to be drawing recruits who have less education, as a recent report documented the percentage of new recruits entering the Army with a high school diploma dropped to a new low. The study, which was conducted by the National Priorities Project (NPP), found slightly more than 70 percent of new recruits joining the active duty Army had a high school diploma, nearly 20 percentage points lower than the Army's goal of at least 90 percent. Army officials confirmed lowering their standards to meet high recruiting goals in the middle of ongoing conflicts that the U.S. was involved in around the world. Massachusetts-based research NPP concluded that the number of high school graduates among new recruits fell to 70.7 percent in 2008. "The trend is clear," Anita Dancs, the project's research director who based the report on Defense Department data released via the Freedom of Information Act, [indicated],"They're missing their benchmarks, and I think it's strongly linked to the impact [of] the Iraq War." The study also found that the number of recruits with both a high school diploma and a score in the upper half on the military's qualification test fell by 15 percent from 2004 to 2007. An analysis of recruiting data revealed that low- and middle-income families are supplying far more Army recruits than families with incomes of more than $60,000 a year.'"

War Pigs: You are Fungible

There are too many War Pigs to count. According to CNN "Former Texas governor Rick Perry wants US troops to go and fight ISIS in the Middle East. He terms the group "the face of evil." Senator Lindsay Graham, a former military litigator, said this at an AIPAC conference, " And if military force is ever employed [against Iran], it should be done in a decisive fashion. The Iranian government's ability to wage conventional warfare against its neighbors and our troops in the region should not exist. They should not have one plane that can fly or one ship that can float." That means that the US "volunteers" will be responsible for eliminating all the Iranians who operate such machinery. One assumes that Graham also thinks no armored vehicles or missile systems or small arms should exist either. The US military would need more than a volunteer force to totally defeat Iran and would c;likely contemplate the use of tactical nuclear weapons. Graham is clearly on the edge of insanity's black hole as are his fellow Hawks.

On that note, American War Pigs want to sell lethal weaponry to its puppet government in Ukraine and actually want to get into combat with Russian troops. Chairman of the US Joint Chiefs of Staff Army General Martin Dempsey said, "I think we should absolutely consider lethal aid..." according to Time Magazine. That means private contractors are needed to sell the machinery and train the Ukrainian personnel.

Women will not long be exempt from Selective Service/Draft registration. It is only the continued dominance of the patriarchs that dominate US society that prevents women from shouldering the burden that men face with their Selective Service responsibility. Sean Kennedy writing for Collegian Central indicated that when Congress lifted the ban on women in combat in 2013, many people expressed concern that the inclusion of women would somehow degrade the quality of our military forces.

Enter US Senator John McCain, War Pig extraordinaire and the the same American representative who glad-handed Ukrainian neo-Nazi and anti-Semite Oleh Tyahnybok in a show of support. "Senator John McCain urged special forces units to ensure that their "rigorous physical standards" are maintained. Never mind that women make up 15 percent of our military or that women have fought for our country as early as the Civil War. While there are certainly physical differences between men and women, the argument that this disparity is enough to warrant the exclusion of women is ludicrous and the perfect example of the mindset we need to distance ourselves from as a country."

Not to worry. If a war with Russia or China breaks out, or with some as yet some unforeseen enemy, McCain and his ilk will be the first to turn to the Selective Service/Draft system to force women to fill the ranks of dead and wounded US military males.

The American war machine is positioning itself for large scale conflict. Every able-bodied American citizen, female and male, will be needed for the carnage.

Just wait and see.

+++++

FIDO and General Wesley Clark in Ukraine: US advisors on the ground with deadly messenger

News that General Wesley Clark, USA (Ret.) visited the Ukraine at the behest of the National Security Advisor there—and also a senior member of Ukraine's parliament—should be a cause for alarm. A nonprofit foundation was involved in this exercise (more below). There is a sense of open, almost joyful viciousness in all this pro-war, anti-Russian sentiments on opinion pages and television broadcasts. It is certainly racist and demeaning in tone. Such is the first step in convincing the public that the "transgressor" is equivalent to a retrovirus.

Interim Report #1: Immediate Improvements Needed in Rapidly Implementing Non-Lethal US Military Assistance for Defense of Ukraine is available at **Cryptome** (and the New York Times) for viewing. General Clark and a former strategy advisor to Secretary of Defense Casper Weinberger named Dr. Phillip Karber, indicates that the two *"participated in 35 meeting [sic] with senior officials, military commanders and various politicians; with Karber visiting front line formations on the Northern, Eastern and Southern Fronts."* The two aging Cold War Warriors recommend immediate shipments of American Body Armor, Night Vision Devices, Communications Equipment, Aviation Fuel and "to maximize their defense potential" Clark and Karber recommend the acquisition of Mig-29's, T-72 tanks, Man-Portable Air Defenses, and Anti-Tank weapons.

Partial expenses for the Clark and Karber expedition were paid for by the Potomac Foundation, a nonprofit foundation in Vienna, Virginia. According to three of its Form 990s, over the years it has received grants from the Smith Richardson Foundation, Soros/Open Society Fund, and Boeing. According to an official at the Potomac Foundation, some support is provided to Georgetown University, in particular, to Karber (**the Chinese Tunnel guy**). The official stated that the group does not have a website.

The Potomac Foundations also runs China Vitae as a charitable activity. According to China Vitae's **website**, it *"was founded in 2001 with two objectives: to raise the quality and quantity of English language, biographical information on China's top leadership; and to create a centralized repository of such information available to a worldwide audience."* China Vitae is run by husband and wife team David and Susan Gries. David Gries is on the board of the Washington Institute for Foreign Affairs and has affiliations with the CIA and Georgetown University. Members listed on the China Vitae website have an assortment of affiliations with universities, corporations and the US government.

The Sith Order returns from the dark side: The general who wanted war with Russia

According to Alexander Cockburn and Jeffrey St. Clair, writing in 1999, General Clark is a madman. *" . . . anyone seeking to understand the bloody fiasco of the Serbian war need hardly look any further than the person of the beribboned Supreme Allied Commander, General Wesley K. Clark . . . A vain, pompous brownnoser, and the poster child for everything that is wrong with the GO (general officer corps) . . ."*

In Wesley Clark: **The Guy Who Almost Started World War III** by Stella Jatras, "No sooner are we told by Britain's top generals that the Russians played a crucial role in ending the West's war against Yugoslavia than we learn that if NATO's supreme commander, the American General Wesley Clark, had had his way, British paratroopers would have stormed Pristina airport, threatening to unleash the most frightening crisis with Moscow since the end of the Cold War. 'I'm not going to start the third world war for you,' General Sir Mike Jackson, commander of the international KFOR peacekeeping force, is reported to have told Gen. Clark when he refused to accept an order to send assault troops to prevent Russian troops from taking over the airfield of Kosovo's provincial capital. The Times of London reported on 23 May 2001 in an article titled, 'Kosovo clash of allied generals,' that 'General Sir Michael Jackson [was] told that he would have to resign if he refused to obey an order by the American commander of NATO's forces during the Kosovo war to stop the Russians from seizing control of Pristina airport in June 1999. If General Clark had had his way, we might have gone to war with Russia, or at least resurrected vestiges of the Cold War and we certainly would have had hundreds if not thousands of casualties in an ill-conceived ground war"

Foreign Internal Defense Operations (FIDO): Standard playbook

Given that US President Obama has blessed the new Kiev government with legitimacy, America now seeks to stabilize the country with infusions of cash, arms and advisors. And that means that FIDO is likely underway there. Former special operations soldiers—now defense contractors—are on the ground in Ukraine, and so are active duty special operators/advisors perhaps out of US Special Operations Command. They are training/tutoring Ukrainian security personnel.

The execution of US national security/military strategy, operations, tactics are very predictable and based on using the impressive US Instruments of National Power to shape the target environment in America's favor. There are many simultaneous operations underway both covert and quite overt. In particular, military information support operations (MISO) begin with manipulating the public consciousness through cyber and meat-space means. That effort is clearly seen in the hyper-hypocritical statements on Russia's annexation of Crimea made by all top national security officials and members of the US Congress. The official words-of-war are gleefully reproduced by the mainstream media and assorted NGO's for a public seemingly unaware or uncaring of such serious international matters. There is **little opposition** to the anti-Russian, pro-war madness.

Then again American infrastructure is crumbling from sea-to-shining sea and so there is a solid rational that can be made for not caring about foreign affairs.

But Americans have seen this movie over and over again since the end of World War II. The script is the same, the bullshit propaganda/myth making is the same, the goals and objectives are the same, and the demonization of the adversary is the same. It is just so formulaic: the USA instigates and creatively destroys; Russia (or any opponent) attempts to counterpunch; China waits for the USA/Russia to commit suicide; and the rest of the world cowers, as they should, selecting to side with whichever one of the three giants can give them the best financial deal or "muscle."

At any rate, according to **Joint Publication 3–22, Foreign Internal Defense**, 12 July 2010, " . . . joint operations, involving the application of all instruments of national power, support host nation efforts to build capability and capacity to free and protect its society from subversion, lawlessness, and insurgency . . . An internal defense and development program (IDAD) program blends four interdependent functions to prevent or counter internal threats. Balanced development attempts to achieve national goals through political, social, and economic programs, allowing all individuals and groups in the society to share in the rewards of development, thus alleviating frustration. The security function includes all activities implemented in order to protect the populace from violence and to provide a safe environment for national development. The security effort should establish an environment in which the HN can provide for its own security with limited US support. Neutralization, a political concept, physically and psychologically separates an insurgent or criminal element from the population, thereby making threatening elements irrelevant to the political process. It includes all lawful measures (except those that degrade the government's legitimacy) to discredit, disrupt, preempt, disorganize, and defeat the insurgent organization. Mobilization provides organized manpower and materiel resources and includes all activities to motivate and organize popular support of the government. Mobilization allows the government to strengthen existing institutions, to develop new ones to respond to demands, and promotes the government's legitimacy . . ."

The ideals stated in the American Declaration of Independence and the US Constitution are currently being crushed by those addicted to warfare, power, money and a view that "they" are the anointed ones, the ones that know what's best for the masses. Great leaders—with all their faults—do not exist any longer in America, nor does a citizenry that vigorously debates and then instructs their representatives to compromise for the sake of the nation, not an ideology. The efforts of George Washington, George C. Marshall, John Adams, Thomas Jefferson, James Madison, Abraham Lincoln and Franklin D. Roosevelt may one day be viewed by future historians and generations as pure folly.

The maniacs are in charge now. "God damn them all to hell!"

+++++

USA a Sinkhole: What's Worth Fighting For?

"Now come on Wall Street don't be slow, why man this war is a-go-go. There's plenty good money to be made, supplying the army

with the tools of the trade. Now come on generals let's move fast, your big chance is here at last. Time you got out and get those Reds, because the only good commie is one that's dead. You know that peace can only be won, when you blow 'em all to kingdom come." — I-Feel-Like-I'm-Fixin'-To-Die Rag, Country Joe and the Fish, 1969

"Corruption is strangling the land. The police force is watching the people, and the people just can't understand. We don't know how to mind our own business, 'cause the whole world's got to be just like us. Now we are fighting a war over there, no matter who's the winner we can't pay the cost. 'Cause there's a monster on the loose, it has got our heads into the noose. And it just sits there watching. America, where are you now, don't you care about your sons and daughters. Don't you know we need you now, we can't fight alone against the Monster." — Monster, Steppenwolf, 1969

First, Reduce the Masses Ability to Reproduce

A nation that refuses to take care of all of its mothers and all of its young children has no future.

"The United States was among just eight countries that experienced an increase in maternal death rates since 2003 – joining countries including Afghanistan and El Salvador....'There's no reason that a country with the resources and the medical expertise that the US has should see maternal deaths going up,' said Dr. Christopher Murray, Director of Institutes for Health Metrics and Evaluation and a co-founder of the Global Burden of Disease. 'The next step would be to examine local-level differences in maternal deaths to look for patterns and the drivers behind those patterns,' reports Jennifer Abel writing in Consumer Affairs. Actually there is a very good reason why the maternal deaths are rising in the USA. Most American leaders really don't care who in America lives or dies—or why--and neither does the bulk of the American population. The elected representatives are merely a reflection of the callous, hollow nature of a long warring republic.

Emergency preparedness is no longer just for the tornado or

snowstorm but for the misery of austerity, job loss, and the aging relative with Alzheimer's who must move home with the newlyweds because federal benefits have been cut, or, more likely, the diversion of more US resources to the nation's national security apparatus and its defense industrial base. Mattress savings techniques are coming back.

If there were fully functional representative democracy in the USA—and with that a coherent US National Security Strategy that includes the health and welfare of its domestic infrastructure and its people—the USA would not be collapsing from within even as it stirs up mayhem, enmity and civil war nearly everywhere around the globe: Ukraine, Georgia, Syria, Afghanistan, Venezuela, Egypt, Pakistan and Xinjiang (PRC) are home to scores of overt and covert US officials, if not activity duty foreign internal defense operators. Dozens of 501C3, not for profit, non-governmental organizations--funded directly by the US government or subsidized indirectly through federal tax exemptions--are a key part of the shape-shifting mix of American ideologues abroad that instigate/lobby for "democracy" in capitals around the world: The Open Society Foundations and the National Endowment for Democracy are two of the most well-known rabble rousers.

It is laughable that they proclaim as their mission "the teaching" of American values to foreigners. More's the pity is the millions of US dollars being given to the usurper government in Ukraine to ensure a "free and fair" election in that country. President Obama says this: "The United States is contributing an $11.4 million package to support the integrity of the May 25 elections. These funds are being used to advance democratic processes – not to support a particular candidate or electoral outcome. These efforts include voter education programs, transparent election administration, effective oversight of the election process, election security and a redress of infractions, and a diverse, balanced and policy-focused media environment." In short, American law firms, press relation groups and assorted consultants will be under contract to make sure the USA gets the outcome it wants in Ukraine. Some of those organizations that have done business in Ukraine are listed in the Foreign Agents Registration database.

Wiley Rein and Tauzin Associates are among them.

Just what are those American values? Maternal death rates on the rise in 2014; 16 million children on some sort of food aid in 2014; 8.2 percent of children born below 2500 grams; 14 percent of Americans unemployed; and crushing debt loads for the bulk of students graduating from America's colleges and universities. One would never know that the USA has severe structural issues with both its physical and mental infrastructure. Yet those problems are normally blamed not on American citizens/government but rather on the Russians, Climate Change, Immigrants, the Chinese, "unqualified American workers," Big Government, and Welfare Moms.

Second, Take Away the People's Livelihood (but legalize pot first)

According to Work in America: Report of a Special Task Force to the Secretary of Health, Education and Welfare (1972): "Our Nation is being challenged by a set of new issues having to do, in one way or another, with the quality of life. This theme emerges from the alienation and disenchantment of blue-collar workers, from the demands of minorities for equitable participation in "the system," from the search by women for a new identity and by the quest of the aged for a respected and useful social role, from the youth who seek a voice in their society, and from almost everyone who suffers from the frustrations of life in a mass society.

Rhetorical, ideological, and partisan responses to these issues abound. But truly effective responses are far more likely to be made if the obscure and complex sources of discontent are sorted out, and the lever of public policy is appropriately placed. Atonie is a condition of deracination--a feeling of rootlessness, lifelessness and dissociation--a word which in the original Greek meant a string that does not vibrate, that has lost its vitality. Besides lending vitality to existence, work helps establish the regularity of life, its basic rhythms and cyclical patterns of day, week, month, and year. Without work, time patterns become confused. One recalls the drifting in T.S. Eliot's The Wasteland: What shall I do. . . .What shall we do tomorrow? What shall we ever do? When duration of unemployment has been prolonged, unemployed workers progress from optimism through pessimism to fatalism. Attitudes toward the future and toward the community and home deteriorate. Children of long-term unemployed and marginally employed workers uniformly show poorer school grades. There are so many unconscious and group needs that work meets that unemployment may lead not only to generalized anxiety, but to free-floating hostility, somatic symptoms and the unconscious selection of some serious illnesses.

Albert Camus wrote that 'Without work all life goes rotten. But when work is soulless, life stifles and dies.' Our analyses of Work in America leads to much the same conclusion: Because work is central to the lives of so many Americans, either the absence of work or employment in meaningless work is creating an increasingly intolerable situation. The human costs of this state of affairs are manifested in worker alienation, alcoholism, drug addiction, and other symptoms of poor mental health. Moreover, much of our tax money is expended in an effort to compensate for problems with at least a part of their genesis in the world of work. A great part of the staggering national bill in the areas of crime and delinquency, mental and physical health, manpower and welfare are generated in our national policies and attitudes towards work."

Third, Create War and Send the People to Fight and Die

Well come on all of you big strong men, Uncle Sam needs your help again. He got himself in a terrible jam, way down yonder in Vietnam. Put down your books and pick up a gun, we're going have a whole lot of fun. And its 1, 2, 3 what are we fighting for? Don't ask me I don't give a damn, the next stop is Vietnam. And its 5, 6, 7 open up the pearly gates. Well there ain't no time to wonder why, we're all going die.— I-Feel-Like-I'm-Fixin'-To-Die Rag, Country Joe and the Fish

+++++

Rockin' in Russia, Murti-Bing Pills in the USA--Trip to Crimea

"The Department of State also warns U.S. citizens to defer all travel to the Crimean Peninsula...Russian forces have occupied the Crimean Peninsula in support of the Russian Federation's claim of Crimean annexation and these forces are likely to continue to take further actions in the Crimean Peninsula consistent with its claim. The United States and Ukraine do not recognize this claimed annexation. The Russian Federation maintains an extensive military presence in Crimea and along the border of eastern Ukraine...Additionally, groups advocating closer ties to Russia have taken on a more strident anti-American tone, especially in eastern Ukraine and Crimea. U.S. citizens who choose to remain in conflict areas should maintain a low profile and avoid large crowds and gatherings." US Department of State, Travel Warning, June 2014.

Imagine the feeling an American might get listening at peak volume to Queen's "We are the Champions and We will Rock You" while driving down the main street of Sevastopol, Crimea-- Federation of Russia-home to the headquarters of the Russian Black Sea flotilla. More on that later.

Insatiability, written in 1927 by Stanislaw Ignacy Witkiewicz, describes a society that is decaying from within whilst from without they face an external threat of "Sino-Mongolian" forces. In Witkiewicz's domestic society, religion, philosophy, politics, art, literature and sex have become devoid of any transcendent qualities. These critical life-moving functions have been twisted into propaganda in order to create disgust for "the other", stir up nationalism and patriotism, and keep the citizens busy. The masses spend their days darting back and forth from one drone-like task to another. Witkiewicz describes them thus, "all those dukes, counts, farmers, peasants, workers, craftsmen, army are vacuous automatons....Because of a spurious sense of social duty and a desire to instruct petty people in petty virtues...whatever appears uncomfortable is either glossed over in silence or else deliberately misconstrued and misinterpreted...What can be expected of the public if the critics themselves are below the average reader?"

Part of the reason for this is to avoid the realities of life by ingesting Murti-Bing pills.

More Zoloft, Crystal Meth Please

"A man who used these Murti-Bing pills changed completely. The problems he had struggled with until then suddenly appeared to be superficial and unimportant. Those once tormented by philosophical insatiability now entered the service of the new society. Instead of writing the dissonant music of former days, they composed marches and odes. Instead of painting abstractions as before, they turned out socially useful pictures," writes Czeslaw Milosz author of the Captive Mind (in his forward to Insatiability). In the end, hooked on Murti-Bing pills, Witkiewicz's characters are, in essence, lobotomized. The characters that Witkiewicz created live dismal lives and are incapable of recognizing that their spirits, souls are bankrupt. "Sturfan wrote abominable things-novels without any heroes, whose role was now assumed by groups...Lilian continued to perform [mechanically] in theater...[They] operated exclusively within the collective psyche, dispensing entirely with dialogue. Art and literary criticism were at last completely abolished."

Witkiewicz's characters no longer refuse--they join, they are indoctrinated by mass audience media and peer pressure and always conform. Indeed, it is far easier and more lucrative to praise and promote the established order than it is to challenge it. The analysts/critics in Insatiability were either employed by organizations who circumscribed their views to preserve the bottom line, or they held a particularly snobbish view of the changing world around them.

Are Americans becoming like the characters in Insatiability or Yevgeny Zamyatin's We? Is the American mass audience media portraying the world in 2014 based on a reality created by American contractors, bureaucrats, technicians, financiers, politicians and academics, rather than the world as it is?

Hazards of Centralized Mass Media

According to the US Army Special Operations Forces Unconventional Warfare guide (2008) the following are the USA's Instruments of National Power (INP's): Diplomacy, Information, Military, Economic, Finance, Law Enforcement and Intelligence. Although all the INP's are critical to American interests (and work in a synergistic fashion), it is the Information section of the INP's that deserves special attention.

The US Army document describes the Information INP this way. "The information environment is the total of individuals, organizations, and systems that collect, process, disseminate, or act on information. The actors include leaders, decision makers, individuals, and organizations. Resources include the materials and systems employed to collect, analyze, apply, or disseminate information. The information environment is where humans and automated systems observe, orient, decide, and act upon information, and is therefore the principal environment of decision making...A medium of information is anything that conveys meaning to a person who perceives the conveyed information. It includes the symbolic meaning perceived in anything taken in by the one who perceives, to include stationary inanimate objects, nature, or man-made images. It also includes messages sent in human interaction-large or small-regardless of whether the message actually delivered was the one intended by the sender or whether the message received was understood as the sender intended. Very broadly, anything and anyone can be an information provider, intentionally or unintentionally."

Freedom to create and disseminate information, whether in print or electronic form, is the direct result of the First Amendment to the US Constitution and the ideals set forth in the Declaration of Independence (various US court cases and Congressional legislation as well). Accuracy and truth in Information is essential particularly as it pertains inside the borders of the United States. According to the Army Special Operations Forces Unconventional Warfare document, "accuracy is distinct because it concerns truth. Truth is a combination of both scientifically verifiable fact and perception...Undemocratic use of media can lead to indoctrination, propaganda, and exploitation.

The US Army Special Operations Forces Unconventional Warfare publication also warns of the dangers of a mass audience media that becomes centralized, collusive and monopolistic. And yet in the USA a relatively small number of corporations in the USA own newspapers, radio stations, publishing houses and television networks, according to Pew's State of the Media. Media power is becoming more centralized at a time when corporations (including media) and the US government have managed to infiltrate and record American life-habits ranging from credit card purchases to telephone conversations. The collected data is used for marketing and behavioral analysis of the American people. No conspiracy here. Edward Snowden's documents released to the journalist Glen Greenwald of the Intercept show the extent to which the US government seeks to know what Americans are thinking and transacting. And, of course, private corporations in the form of defense contractors and telecommunications giants are in on the gig.

Trust Us

The two primary, semi-official US government/corporate organs *The Washington Post* and *The New York Times* have often lent their services/journalism to America's intelligence agencies, particularly during the Cold War. On the overt front, Washington Post owner Jeff Bezos' company Amazon has a newly minted $600 million dollar contract with the Central Intelligence Agency to improve its computing operation. NNDB.com has this to say about famed Washington Post national security reporter Walter Pincus. "According to published reports, Pincus worked for the CIA during the early 1960s, though whenJohn Deutch was asked directly if Pincus was an 'asset', he claimed not, but did express familiarity with the non-asset. The CIA did pay for him to attend two overseas conferences by Pincus' own 1967 admission. The *Washington Times* (a Moon publication) on 31 July 1996 described Pincus by saying that "some in the agency refer to [Pincus] as 'the CIA's house reporter'".

Carl Bernstein reported that American journalism and intelligence operations fit hand-in-glove. "The use of journalists has been among the most productive means of intelligence gathering employed by the CIA...By far the most valuable of these associations, according to CIA officials, have been with the *New York Times,* CBS and Time Inc." With America over a decade into a worldwide war on terror, and, by design, headed into a next generation Cold War with Russia and China, one can only speculate how many journalists are being recruited to work with the CIA.

If the mass audience media, telecommunications providers/ISP's, content providers and social media companies work on and off with the US national security establishment and corporate marketers to promote the fashion or war of the day, does American really have a "free" press?

As Americans move from early youth on to later years, they increasingly define themselves through interaction with a spectrum of content transmitted via human-to-human, electronic, print and symbolic mediums as indicated in the Army Special Operations Unconventional Warfare document. Americans see themselves in technology, in automobiles, in the latest fashion, in fictional characters on television or the movie screen, in the liberal and conservative opinions of academics and commentators, or the favored professional sports franchise marketed by a corporation.

USA Favors Cold War America

This forces questions: What is an American? Who, really, are "you"? Are "you" merely the sum of what others want "you" to be, to wear and eat? Do "you" believe the rationale for more American military, intelligence and contractor intervention on land, sea (and under it), air and space? Do "you" know anything about the world other than searching the World Wide Web? Is the information you depend on to define "yourself" true and accurate?

According to the US Army Special Operations Forces

Unconventional Warfare publication, the "hazards of centralized mass media include the following: A disproportion of power occurs. Disproportionate informational power accrues to those who control centralized mass media; arguably, it is inherently undemocratic. An inability to transmit tacit knowledge--the context of content presented must either be explicitly explained or is assumed to be understood by the receiver. A focus on the unusual and sensational to capture the receivers' attention, leading to a distortion and trivialization of reality. The deliberate promotion of emotions such as anxiety, fear, or greed can be used to sell a particular agenda. An inability to deal with complex issues because of time and economic constraints leads to simplification, further distorting and trivializing reality...Democratic and independent use of media theoretically serves to educate the public or electorate about issues regarding government and society."

The United States now, arguably, has a centralized media that has no inhibitions about pushing a view of the world outside US borders because it is good for business. The American public is being misinformed about a world that has largely moved beyond Cold War thinking and action. Indeed the rapidity with which China, Russia and Turkey have absorbed "the American way of life" and Western European fashion/culture/music is astonishing. They have adapted "us" to "them" so to speak. Ironically, the USA is engaging in the sort of rhetoric used by the former USSR which tried and failed to convince the world of Western decadence. Russia is evil, China is evil, the Axis of Evil is evil. It is absurd.

Learning and Partying in Russia

Consider Moscow, Russia. Think of a combination of Houston, Texas; Chicago, Illinois and New York City all merged together. Ford, Chevy, BMW, Mercedes, Honda and Hyundai automobiles populate their roads. Drivers are on mobiles devices from Apple I-Phones to Samsung mobiles. The autobahn that encircles Moscow is jammed with vehicles cutting in and out of traffic at high speeds. Traffic jams are common even at 10:30 pm on a Sunday (it is light until nearly 11:00 pm). There are no noticeable speed limit signs or speed traps. It is a drag race where one has to be supremely confident in speed racing. American conservatives and liberals would not know what to make of this "freedom" to get where one needs to get without having to worry about a speeding ticket which finds its origin in a severe regulatory regime.

Moscow is a gritty city. Some describe it as dirty but that is incorrect. Building facades are not something the Russians are concerned with. So they are dusty, apparently not maintained. But enter what looks to be a crummy shopping Mall, or an apartment, and the interiors are well-kept (one such Mall was similar to Pentagon City).

Sevastopol, Simferopol and Yalta on the Crimean coastline are beautiful, tastefully constructed and clean with fine highway systems and reliable mass transit. The longest electric trolley bus service in Russia runs from Simferopol to Yalta. Those communities have the most beautiful women in the world, even beyond Tel Aviv's.

Young children (and families) were everywhere to be seen in the Crimea (in Moscow too). Sevastopol and Yalta were packed with tourists from all over Russia celebrating Russian Independence Day. World War II and Crimean War remembrances were included in that three day holiday event and mixed with celebrations that included traditional music and dance, patriotic songs, and rock and jazz concerts. Beer dominates and is for sale 24/7. Burger King in Sevastopol advertises a meal not with a Coke but with a beer. On that note, Coke, Pepsi and Budweiser can be purchased with ease.

Business was brisk along the Crimean boardwalks (made of concrete and granite) in spite of US sanctions. It is a carnival of sorts similar to the scene at the fish market in Seattle in Washington State, USA. Visa and Mastercard function in Crimea. The banking system of Crimea has collapsed, for the moment, so paper money is used for many transactions. Cruise ship tours to Crimea have ceased due to economic sanctions and Western Union money transfers can't be made there, but the Russians take it all in stride. As one Russian remarked, "They will come back in time.

Life moves."

There were no tanks, no armored vehicles, no soldiers or police lining the public roads. Only at Simferopol International Airport could many security personnel be seen. Interested in see the warship Moscow and other military vessels in port? Negotiate for a private boat tour and take a picture, up close. Want to travel into a former USSR nuclear submarine pen where the seriousness of the Cold War comes to life? Get over to Balaclava and walk the miles of concrete and marvel at the construction (which must mirror US submarine pens of the era). The site of the Charge of the Light Brigade took place not far from the site of the Cold War submarine base.

Vineyards populate the island of Crimea and the wine there is tops. And there are 2500 BCE year old Greek and Roman ancient ruins to be discovered. Orthodox Russian churches and cathedrals dot the landscape and anyone is welcome to walk in and light a candle for a minimal fee. But the character and strength of the Russian people is, as Vasily Grossman wrote in the novel Life and Fate, their faith in "simple acts of kindness", and their history and the ties that bind them to their ground, their piece of the Earth. "People are basically the same everywhere. Marketing is the same everywhere. Politics is the same everywhere. Freedom comes from within and if you don't know where you come from and belong and you can't change and you can't discover yourself, life will be miserable for you," said a Yalta barkeeper.

The USA is an exceptional country and one worth arguing for. But the USA has become a conventional, conservative behemoth stuck in a Cold War exceptionalist mindset. Americans can't seem to accept their "victory" in the Cold War. In so many ways the world has adopted the "American way of life" to suit their unique cultures. And it's not about "loving or leaving the USA." But it most certainly is about fixing the USA so one love's to come back to it without disillusionment. So Americans will have to decide what kind of people they want to remain as or advance to. They will have to take it upon themselves to become informed.

As Czeslaw Milosz puts it, "Perhaps sunlight, the smell of the earth, little everyday pleasures and the forgetfulness that work brings can ease somewhat the tensions created by this process...But beneath the activity and bustle of daily life is the constant awareness of an irrevocable choice to be made. One must either die--physically or spiritually--or else one must be reborn according to the prescribed method; namely, the taking of Murti-Bing pills. People in the [USA] are often inclined to consider the lot of converted countries in terms of might and coercion. That is wrong. There is an internal longing for harmony and happiness that lies deeper than the ordinary fear of the desire to escape misery or physical destruction."

Oh, I almost forgot, it was awesome listening to Queen's "We are the Champions" and "We will Rock You" while racing in a Japanese car down the main road in Sevastopol, the home of the Russian Black Sea flotilla.

 It was like being home in the USA. But there is no place like home.

+++++

Baghdadi, Obama, Netanyahu, Porashenko and Abe: The Five Fingers of Death

"You know, they're schemers: Schemers trying to control their worlds. I'm not a schemer. I try to show the schemers how pathetic their attempts to control things really are...You know what, you know what I noticed? Nobody panics when things go according to plan: Even if the plan is horrifying. If tomorrow I tell the press that like a gang banger will get shot, or a truckload of soldiers will be blown up, nobody panics, because it's all part of the plan." — Heath Ledger's Joker, the Dark Knight, 2008.

"They did not repent of their murders, their sorcery, their immorality, or of their thefts."— Revelations

There will be no such event called the Third World War as humanity is still playing out World War I, World War II and the Cold War. The leaders referenced in the title of this article are, or will be, the primary instigators for continued waves of carnage around the globe. Their statements, executive decisions and political/military actions affect the lives of nearly every soul on Earth.

Surprise Attack!

If Japan's Prime Minister Shinzo Abe has is way, the Japanese military will start producing and fielding nuclear weapons. It will purchase more weaponry from the United States and enhance its defense industrial base to produce its own war making equipment. The rationale for these actions is China's emergence as a world power. Already Abe has stirred up memories of WWII and has publicly attempted to glorify the actions of Japanese soldiers during that conflict. Abe also oversaw a revision to Japan's constitution opening the door for preemptive military action by Japanese forces. China has a vivid memories of Japanese soldiers raping and slaughtering women and children, young and old in Nanjing.

"Japanese Prime Minister Shinzo Abe spent two full days in the resource-rich South Pacific nation of Papua New Guinea last Friday and Saturday, underscoring the geo-strategic ambitions behind his government's decision to 're-interpret' Japan's constitution to enable the country's armed forces to engage in overseas military operations…he clearly glorified the military campaigns of World War II. According to the Japanese public broadcaster NHK World, Abe said Japan's present-day prosperity was based on the troops who sacrificed their lives."

The world is now seeing the 21st Century version of Nanjing as Israel has slaughtered-at-a-distance close to 1,000 Palestinians in Gaza. Israel has suffered 30 casualties soldiers. Most of the Palestinians murdered have been women and children, done in by

Israeli soldiers flying American made aircraft and ordnance. President Obama and America's political and military leaders have taken an "oh-well" view of this matter which one more phase of the Israeli scheme to eliminate the Palestinians and take there land and resources. Some call this genocide . The United States supports this action just as it supported the coups in Ukraine and Egypt. Clearly the nation's priorities are twisted particularly with Israel. When the primer minister of Israel receives more standing ovations and applause from a joint session of the US Congress than the President of the United states, that's the "tail wagging the dog." And again we are reminded that Israel was a child of WWII.

When will there be a Real War? I want my Fulda Gap!

US President Barack Obama is overseeing a war against Russia in Eastern Ukraine and via international economic sanctions overseen by the US Treasury Department. Obama has openly stated that he will be sending US military advisers to support Ukraine's military operations against pro-Russian rebels in Eastern Ukraine's breakaway republics. But they are already there operating under the Foreign Internal Defense Operations policy and practice manual. And, if the US military and intelligence community is doing operations the right way, teams of CIA paramilitary and special operations operatives have been forward observing in Russia. At any rate America's newest puppet, who will legitimize US military activity on Russia's border, is Petro Porashenko put into office thanks to a successful US-backed coup against the former president Viktor Yanukovych. Porashenko leads a ragtag government of wealthy interests and neo-Nazi groups whose support is based largely in Western Ukraine.

The destruction of Malaysia flight MH17 over Eastern Ukraine has been used as a political football by the USA and its allies to demonize Russia and lay the blame for the tragedy at the doorstep of Russia's president Vladimir Putin. Somehow the Russian government is responsible for the deaths of 292 people because it supports the pro-Russian rebels in their fight against US backed thugs in Ukraine. Duh, what are they supposed to do? What will the US do when splinter groups in Mexico, supported by the

Mexican government, cross the unto the USA and start placing IED's in cities and towns in Arizona and Texas?

The USA remains upset because Russia moved to take back Crimea before the USA could get its hands on it and derail plans by Russia, China and the European Union to integrate by rail, pipelines, ports and highways many of the economies of Asia and Europe. Ultimately, the people of Crimea voted overwhelmingly in a referendum to join the Russian Federation.

Looking around at world events it is hard not to seek guidance from character portrayals in the movies or biblical scripture. People in the "real" world , particularly the impact leaders named in the title of this article, are the 21st Century versions of Timur (Tamerlane) who is said to have killed 17 million people or 5 percent of the world's population. He sought to reestablish the Mongol empire of Genghis Khan. In like manner, members of the Five Fingers of Death are indifferent to the suffering, slaughter and displacement of their own populations, and those of other nations. The political/military leadership in the United States and the European Union—and their mouthpieces in the media—are maniacal cartoon characters who fancy themselves as some sort of a combination of Tamerlane, Cicero, Frederick the Great, Sun Tzu and Clausewitz. They seek Big War with China and Russia. World War II, the Korean War and Iraq and Afghanistan were not enough. Indeed, the War on Terror infuriates them because it is not a "real fight" like a full-scale war with "real military and economic powers."

Hit Me Like a Diamond Bullet

The Islamic Caliphate led by Baghdadi apparently has studied history. Who would have guessed that ***Down with the 1916*** Sykes Picot ***Agreement!*** would be a rallying cry for the front line soldiers of the Islamic Caliphate? The Islamic Caliphate is a ruthless and brilliant organization. Colonel Kurtz, played by Marlon Brando in the movie Apocalypse Now, describes them accurately: "I remember when I was with Special Forces… seems a thousand centuries ago. We went into a camp to inoculate some children.

We left the camp after we had inoculated the children for polio, and this old man came running after us and he was crying. He couldn't see. We went back there, and they had come and hacked off every inoculated arm. There they were in a pile. A pile of little arms. And I remember... I... I... I cried, I wept like some grandmother. I wanted to tear my teeth out; I didn't know what I wanted to do! And I want to remember it. I never want to forget it... I never want to forget. And then I realized... like I was shot... like I was shot with a diamond... a diamond bullet right through my forehead. And I thought, my God... the genius of that! The genius! The will to do that! Perfect, genuine, complete, crystalline, pure. And then I realized they were stronger than we, because they could stand that these were not monsters, these were men... trained cadres. These men who fought with their hearts, who had families, who had children, who were filled with love... but they had the strength... the strength... to do that. If I had ten divisions of those men, our troubles here would be over very quickly. You have to have men who are moral... and at the same time who are able to utilize their primordial instincts to kill without feeling... without passion... without judgment... without judgment! Because it's judgment that defeats us. "

The Islamic Caliphate should be judged carefully. It exists for many reasons. The obvious ones are America's support for the overthrow of the Syrian government of president Bashar Al-Assad; America's strategy of arming Al Qaeda splinter groups, with funding provided by Saudi Arabia, to fight the Syrian army; America's strategy of eliminating Assad to deny Russia and Iran a significant ally; the ongoing indigenous religious and civil war between Shia and Sunni taking place in Syria, Iraq, Bahrain, Yemen and elsewhere; and America's invasion of Iraq which destabilized the entire Middle East.

Baghdadi's stroke of genius was to proclaim himself above all other Muslim leaders. Why? The answer to that is because the wealthy rulers/leaders of Saudi Arabia, Jordan, Egypt, Iraq and Syria have done little to provide employment, food and shelter to the millions that make up their populations. The unemployment rate of the youth of those countries, according to Al Arabiya, is a staggering 23 percent. In addition American military operations–or those supported by the USA–have caused millions to be displaced within Iraq and Syria and into refugee camps in Turkey, Iran, Jordan and Lebanon (the Christian communities in these countries have nearly been eliminated) And what more can be said about the suffering of he Palestinians? Arab leaders have used the Palestinians as pawns opting for the status quo of pain.

The Islamic Caliphate understand these matters well. Their actions and statements indicate that they are disgusted with all the duplicity and ineffectiveness of Arab governments and Muslim leaders the world over. They mean to take the fight to the false prophets of Islam and to the corporate religion of Capitalism. In so doing they are inviting the world to their back yard for a battle. And they are likely planning for attacks inside the United States, Europe, Arab capitals and Israel. Their fighters are mobile traveling from North Africa, Chechnya, Saudi Arabia, Afghanistan, Iraq, and Yemen to engage their foes.

They also know that consequences of American strategy, operations and tactics in the Middle East, and Persian Gulf regions: The creation of millions refugees and internally displaced persons– ideal recruits. They pose enticing questions to those unemployed and the Arab world at large: "What has the government done for you? What have the leaders of Islam done for the poor, unemployed, disenfranchised and displaced? You have no prospects for work or education or even a purpose." "Come join us," they say. "We offer you the chance to fight and destroy these devious forces. You will know what camaraderie is for the first time. We will clothe, feed, arm and train you. The days will be harsh but rewarding. If you die, you will be martyr of the cause and never be forgotten."

Let a Thousand Bilateral Agreements Bloom

Challenges to the post WWII financial system are threaten America's financial and economic Instruments of National Power. The BRICS have openly challenged elements of that system—IMF and World Bank–recently by rolling out their own version of those two institutions. But that is not the most interesting move by China and fellow BRICS members. Peter Lee makes the point:

"The United States is backing off from its stated 'honest broker' position in the South China Sea to a tilt toward China's adversaries, offering the possibility of direct confrontation over the PRC's maritime claims and use of the sanctions regime to punish PRC misbehavior…. So the PRC internationalizes the yuan in a series of bilateral agreements with key trading partners, so that its financial transactions increasingly exit the dollar and are less vulnerable to US and Western sanctions; it tries to push its investors to look for adequate returns in friendly regions rather than dumping excess funds in Western financial centers…And the Xi Jinping regime must take into account the possibility that the outrage and sanctions machine, so intensively deployed against Russia over Ukraine, will be employed against the People's Republic of China…"

Why the twin-fetish's with Russia and China? Why the "holier than thou" egomania of US policy makers? Is it the curriculum and teaching methodologies at America's elite universities? West Point (General Stanley McChrystal)? Harvard and Yale (Barack Obama and Samantha Power)? Stanford (Condi Rice and Susan Rice)? Princeton (General David Petraeus)? Who knows? There are many similar to these folks from hundreds of lower caliber universities.

One thing for certain though: However they make their way to the US President's ear, thinks tanks, opinion pages, the corporate boardroom or university professorship, they are the Messiahs of American Exceptionalism. They are placed into positions of power and influence by those who came before (Cold Warriors and their apostles) and were "produced" and selected to "lead" the country. They are funneled into political, media, academic military and economic positions of influence in government and industry. They are inter-changeable parts of the American national security machinery: On one day they are defending the US constitution; on another sitting on a corporate board pulling in $100,000 (US), or commenting on the latest disaster on newscasts.

Humanity Flushing Itself Down the Toilet

The first decades of the 21st Century were predicted by politicians, economists and pundits to be the start of a new era of creative Capitalism, empowering technologies, and belief in the good faith and credit of the world's American-backed financial system. Some social scientists proclaimed that the global wars of the 20th Century would remain confined to that century and have no place in the 21st Century. It's not working out that way.

Humanity is the creation of the cosmos, local and universal; in particular, the interactions between geography, climate, culture and human/nonhuman generated events. History is the reporting done to explain to current and future generations what human actors, individually or as a collective, were doing at some point in time. "Everything flows," as Vasily Grossman, the author of a book of the same name, once said. History is not unlike the Nile River or the Mississippi River with dozens of tributaries, streams, and unseen aquifers affecting the main body of the river. In short every person, place or thing is connected in some fashion to the flow of life, of history. And each person will, at some point in a lifetime, be affected by what has taken place 10, 20 or 100 years ago.

Humanity has no learned much it seems. We have learned how to kill and communicate faster. We live longer but for what purpose? World War I began 100 years ago this August, 2014. World War II ended just 70 years ago. The Cold War and those two World Wars are with us still. Consider this: The USA still operates under the Carter Doctrine: " An attempt by any outside force to gain control of the Persian Gulf region will be regarded as an assault on the vital interests of the United States. It will be repelled by the use of any means necessary, including military force."

American presidents Jimmy Carter and Ronald Reagan approved the training and arming of Islamic fundamentalists to fight the Russians in Afghanistan and instigate, or carry out, violent acts in the former Soviet republics. Pakistan was critical in this effort. Operation Cyclone was one such operation that took place in Afghanistan in the grand theater that was the Cold War. Al-Qaeda was formed amidst the conflict between the USA and USSR.

Operation Cyclone's driving force was Michael Vickers, born during the Cold War in 1953. He is currently the US Defense Department's Undersecretary of Defense for Intelligence. His official US Department of Defense biography notes with some bravado that "During the mid-1980s, Secretary Vickers was the principal strategist for the largest covert action program in the CIA's history: the paramilitary operation that drove the Soviet army out of Afghanistan."

The rest is history.

+ + + + +

American Defense Contractors are now Health Care Providers: Tracking Patient Data Like Tracking a Missile

"Defense Contractor" is no longer a valid term for US weapons makers.

References to the "military industrial complex" are agonizingly silly particularly since the man who coined the term --President Dwight Eisenhower--was as ruthless as his CIA director John Foster Dulles. According to the Miller Center at the University of Virginia, defense spending never fell below 50 percent of the US budget during Eisenhower's presidency. In fact, he increased spending on nuclear weapons. And it gets worse:

"During his first year in office, Eisenhower authorized the CIA to deal with... Iran that had begun during Truman's presidency. In August 1953, the CIA helped overthrow [Iran's] government and restore the shah's power. In the aftermath of this covert action, new arrangements gave U.S. corporations an equal share with the British in the Iranian oil industry. He relied frequently on covert action to avoid having to take public responsibility for controversial interventions... CIA tactics were sometimes unsavory, as they included bribes, subversion, and even assassination attempts. But Eisenhower authorized those actions, even as he maintained plausible deniability, that is, carefully concealing all evidence of U.S. involvement so that he could deny any responsibility for what had happened...A year later, the CIA helped overthrow the elected government of Guatemala..."

Multi-Service Contractors

So diverse in expertise ranging from intelligence, surveillance, reconnaissance, energy management, nuclear power, space launch systems and health care solutions it is futile to maintain the illusion that American defense contractors build only killing machines. The evidence clearly shows that these companies straddle the commercial and government divide; hence, it is more appropriate to term them Multi-Service Contractors (MSC's). So critical is war preparation and making for advances in US information and health care technologies that the MSC's actually have an advantage over many private corporations unable to transfer battlefield innovations into useful technology products that can be used by, say, hospitals and insurance companies.

That is why Lockheed can unabashedly claim that tracking patient and healthcare data is like tracking a missile, Lockheed Martin's Health and Life Sciences division offers products for genomics, patient big data tracking and analysis, and sepsis monitoring. According to Lockheed's website :

" Using analytical technology developed to detect launched missiles, Lockheed Martin has discovered a way to identify sepsis, a potentially fatal blood condition, between 14 to 16 hours earlier than physicians currently do. The solution requires looking at the human body's data the same way you would collect sensor data from a missile traveling at mach speed – as continuously changing signals. Initial trials indicate Lockheed Martin's solution detects Sepsis, a leading cause of death in the U.S., faster and more accurately than current industry-accepted methods."

The kill/pacify chain is now invoked not to signify the process to kill, capture of pacify an individual or collective human enemy, it is to describe a process to identify, terminate or manage the disease/illness within an individual patient or a group of patients. Find, fix, track, target, engage, assess. Deadly microorganisms are now as evil as the Islamic State terrorists.

So Lockheed Martin and Northrop Grumman have made nearly complete their transition to bona fide national health care providers. The makers of the F-35 and Unmanned Aerial Vehicles like Global Hawk and X47-B UCAS are now defending the health and wellness of the American civilian population. So, in a sense, it's a homeland security mission: what could be worse for national security than a sickly American public, particularly one that needs to be fit to fight the war on terror and potentially Russia and China.

As Northrop Grumman puts it:

"Northrop Grumman sustains the essential functions of population health with reliable and responsive technologies. We embrace the health protection mission across domestic and global customer partnerships, and are committed to strengthening their response to challenges. Years of experience in public health help drive the quality of our population health solutions and services – which enable the characterization of population health risks, projected health costs and potential savings. The systems we support have been pivotal in every major health-related event in recent years – from natural disasters like Hurricane Katrina to disease outbreaks like H1N1."

But it is not just the behemoths of the American defense industrial base that have found profits in the health services and medical support industry, it's comparatively smaller defense contractors like Blue Canopy LLC-- that serves the US Defense Intelligence Agency and "other classified" customers along with a small slate of commercial enterprises--that have become, like the giants of defense contracting, legitimate players in the health care industry.

Visit http://oig.hhs.gov/oei/reports/oei-03-14-00231.pdf: "An Overview of 60 Contracts…" and perform web searches on the contractors listed in the report by the inspector general at the Department of Health and Human Services. Defense contractors figure prominently.

War is Healthy

And there should be no surprise at these developments. America is a nation at war, still operating under the 911 state of emergency. The prime mover behind the creation of the US Constitution, former American president James put it:

"Of all the enemies to public liberty war is, perhaps, the most to be dreaded, because it comprises and develops the germ of every other. War is the parent of armies; from these proceed debts and taxes; and armies, and debts, and taxes are the known instruments for bringing the many under the domination of the few. In war, too, the discretionary power of the Executive is extended; its influence in dealing out offices, honors, and emoluments is multiplied; and all the means of seducing the minds, are added to those of subduing the force, of the people. The same malignant aspect in republicanism may be traced in the inequality of fortunes, and the opportunities of fraud, growing out of a state of war, and in the degeneracy of manners and of morals engendered by both. No nation could preserve its freedom in the midst of continual warfare."

On that note do yourself a favor and purchase Michael Glennon's National Security and Double Government. The book by the Tufts University professor is an excellent piece of sober scholarship. As Glennon states in the work, " The public believes that constitutionally established institutions control national security policy--but that view is mistaken."

So the next time you find yourself in the hospital or under treatment by a physician, thank your lucky stars for perpetual war and the efforts of America's MSC's.

+++++

The American Education System: Critical Capitalist Infrastructure, Ignorant Adults

"In times of rapid change, the learners inherit the earth, while the learned find themselves beautifully equipped to deal with a world that no longer exists." *Eric Hoffer*

"Every valuable human being must be a radical and a rebel, for what he must aim at is to make things better than they are." *Neils Bohr*

"A good case can be made for ending initial education (more of which could be obtained in the home through electronic devices) somewhere around the age of eighteen. This formal initial period could be followed by two years of service in a socially desirable cause; then by direct involvement in some professional activity and by advanced, systematic training within that area; and finally by regular periods of one and eventually even two years of broadening, integrative study at the beginning of every decade of one's life, somewhere up to the age of sixty." *Zibignew Brezezinski 1970*

There is an illuminating briefing produced by the Center for Digital Education titled Education Market Forecast, 2012. One page, in particular, displays where select US K-12 schools and universities would rank in the Fortune 500. The New York City K-12 school system, with US $18.5 billion in revenue, would be ranked number 136 far ahead of Marriot International and Yahoo, Inc. At the college level, the University of Michigan with US $5.8 billion in revenue ranks ahead of MasterCard and the Washington Post.

There are approximately 4,493 colleges and universities in the USA with some 35 million or so students. At the K-12 level there are roughly 49 million students in 98,708 public school facilities in 14,000 districts. Private schools (parochial, charter, etc.) have nearly 6 million students under their care in as many as 33,000 facilities. States of the United States spent (all sources) nearly US $2 trillion on education. K-12 and college/university systems employ 11.1 million people. Only 50 percent of the 11.1 million are teachers with the other 50 percent being administrators, ground and maintenance personnel, technology advisors, etc. It is worth noting that public and private spending (all sources) on the

K-12 through the college and university levels in the United States exceeds that spent on social security and national defense combined.

"Colleges and universities are important regional economic engines for their communities and are multifaceted in that they provide education, workforce training, employment, research activity, and health care," according to Moody's Education Outlook 2012. It is becoming the case that colleges and universities are employers of last resort in places like Detroit, Michigan or Up State New York. This is likely to change for the worse as in January 2013 Moody's indicated in its US Higher Education Outlook Negative for 2013 that "the US higher education sector has hit a critical juncture in the evolution of its business model."

Education Factories

Mark Twain, Thoreau, Shakespeare, Diversity and Sustainability notwithstanding, the American education system (K-12, college/university) is a profit making industry (despite the org/edu claims) that is in the business of manufacturing, and warehousing, American human capital. Any nation-state that hopes for longevity must design an education system that ensures a secure life and continuity for its people. That means teaching national/social uniformity in living and purpose.

The US education system is the backbone, the spinal column of the nation.

A key function of the education industry is to develop and produce taxpayers that will have skillsets useful in maintaining and increasing the nation's productivity levels whether in a research laboratory or the bedroom (nation's fertility rate). Critical in the manufacturing process is designing individual and collective minds to agree to the covenant, a sort of the secular religion, between "we the people" and the US Constitution, the Bill of Rights and the ideals contained in the Declaration of Independence. Those same minds are manufactured to generally accept the worldviews of American business, education and government leaders flowing through corporate media.

Another critical function of the US education industry is to produce minds that are numb to the contradictions in the capitalist, globalist mode of living and thinking. Certainly not numb to asking questions of the system (to a point); but produced with an inability to think with depth and breadth about the globalized world, about life and one's place in it, about connections. In 1950 Dean Acheson once remarked that higher order Americans spend about 10 minutes a day thinking about what goes on outside the borders of the USA. Even with the Internet and WWW, that 10 minute mark probably still holds.

From preschool to graduate school students undergo a form of distraction therapy. Video games, American Idol, late night talk shows, nonsense news and information, marketers for clothing, tech gear, music, and credit cards bombard the mind like spray wax at the end of a car wash. But this is all part of the plan for education in America. It's an education in buying and selling; what George W. Bush described as freedom, "freedom is the ability to buy and sell." He was right on many levels but no one likes to pull the curtain back and find that the education industry is just like the defense industry with contractors, consultants, presidents, CEO's, analysts, investment bankers, fraud, waste, abuse etc.

It is utterly popular and awfully tedious to say that there is an education-military complex. Eisenhower's overused statement is very much dated. In fact President U.S. Grant thought about those matters during his presidency. But, we seem to be in the midst of the development of a national security republic perpetually at war and undereducated, by design, in the machinations of the American national security state.

Arguably, it is dangerous to try and break up the industrial model of education, particularly now in the midst of high unemployment in the USA and the perilous state of the US and world economy. The warehousing function that K-12 and college universities play is vital to local economies and keeping millions of young people off the street. The industrial model excels at manufacturing minds with conformity/uniformity built in.

And yet, the US education industry is not even listed as a leading

Critical Infrastructure sector in the USA. Perhaps it should be listed under the Defense Industrial Base as important as its function is to the nation.

What's a Nation State to Do?

So you want to privatize, corporatize, and decentralize the US education industry? You want to end formalized education at 18 years of age as Brezezinski said in 1970? Is this the best way to get more competent American engineers, scientists, warfighters, buyers, and sellers? You want to make the US education industry more efficient and effective? You want high scores on the national College Board-Educational Testing Service (teach to the test) to claim the number one slot in the world? You want to save money by eliminating excess human capital, and closing/consolidating schools? You want to do Podcasts, Skype around the world, work in electronic collectives via the Internet and World Wide Web?

The answers to these questions raise significant issues for the future stability of the American nation-state and, indeed, the continuity of the American Republic and its form of government. At the moment, the glue that binds Americans together is many years of participation in the US education educational system.

What needs to be changed within the American education is not so much the addition of technical wizardry, robust communications networks, or the next big fad (teacher as facilitator, blended learning, TED lectures, etc.). An emphasis needs to be placed on the nuts and bolts, the blocking and tackling aspects of education, the items that are foundational—human capital.

It all has to start with the reeducation of "educated" adults in positions of power: parents, professors, teachers, mentors, politicians, military leaders, et al. It is a crime to blame the young for the failings, the ignorance, of adults who refuse to re-educate themselves about the world around them. They fear the information and knowledge that the Internet and WWW. They are the "learned" that Eric Hoffer refers to above.

Duh...What?

Most American adults do not know the difference between the Internet and WWW or have a rudimentary knowledge of the history and mechanics behind it. Hence, the young reflect that. The same adults would not be able to locate Benin or Brunei on a map even though Google Earth is at their fingertips. "I know nothing about anatomy," said an adult recently. Well, over at Chrome there are, for no charge but time, 3D software programs on human anatomy. In fact, for every field of academic endeavor, there is a free education software program that can be downloaded and used to self-educate.

Over 50 percent of American adults reject Evolutionary Theory and Evolutionary Psychology/Biology. American adults (the "great leaders") are destroying America's English language to the point that words/concepts like accountability, torture, displaced peoples, drones, casualties, shootings and death are meaningless to K-12 and college university students. Those same adults rip teachers and administrators for lack of effort and appropriate qualifications and demand action and accountability.

Finally, the academic disciplines are mostly stove-piped and isolated from each other during a time when understanding the economic, social, biological, and cultural interconnections from the local to global level are paramount. In fact, students are more stimulated and thrive in a well-run interdisciplinary program as opposed to smokestack pedagogy. There are many ways to discover. For example, can literary analysis/criticism inform about militarism in society? Yes. Greg Winston's Joyce and Militarism (2012, University of Florida) focuses in on some of James Joyce's classics and the times/environment they were written. It is an extraordinary book that travels through the occupation of Ireland by England and World War I.

Murray Gell Mann put it best at a conference sponsored by the National Defense University in 2003.

"Unfortunately, in a great many places in our society, including academia and most bureaucracies, prestige accrues principally to those who study carefully some aspect of a problem, while discussion of the big picture is relegated to cocktail parties. It is of crucial importance that we learn to supplement those specialized studies with what I call a crude look at the whole...It is essential, in my opinion, to make some effort to search out in advance what kinds of paths might lead humanity to a reasonably sustainable and desirable world during the coming decades. And while the study of the many different subjects involved is being pursued by the appropriate specialists, we need to supplement that study with interdisciplinary investigations of the strong interdependence of all the principal facets of the world situation. In short, we need a crude look at the whole, treating global security and global politics as parts of a very general set of questions about the future."

What a radical idea.

+++++

America's Threat Centric Education System: Out of Date and Out of Time

"History is a story. That's why we fight over history. We make sense of ourselves, the world and ourselves in the world through the struggle to tell the truth through stories. Facts have to be contextualised to become the truth. And that truth is a struggle that is constantly fought over. It is not given. And telling stories helps to create debate about that truth. That is why working people should tell their stories. Truth is a class issue. I would appeal to all your readers, especially to young ones, to make their own political films; shoot interviews, especially with older comrades, and dare to express themselves on the screen. Film making is for everybody. I would be looking at the new technologies. They are disruptive and a problem in capitalist society…That's why they want to close down the Internet if they can. Politicians don't like allowing people to communicate anonymously with each other. They want to restrain freedom … But still for a while there is a window of opportunity and freedom. They monitor you, but don't yet stop you. That will come, of course…[But] it's where people ought to be, where creative people and political people ought to be." *Tony*

Garnett interviewed by the editors of WSWS

How can young people be encouraged and coached to narrate a "true" history of their lives and times in the world—and the events, people and geography that influence them—for the bulk of their literate existence (i.e., 21st Century literate to include visual and technological literacy)? How can they be motivated to bypass the standard historical corporate media sanctioned fare of Steven Ambrose, Doris Kearns-Goodwin or David McCullough? How can they be motivated to collaborate and push against forces that seek to program them to accept "austerity" and "it is what it is"? How can America's threat-centric, industrial education system be changed?

The answer to those questions is in the hands of many in America's legacy generation who have sickened on the state of American education, now a mish-mash of public, private and charter schools each on its own divergent mission. They clap and cheer at the latest TED speech, or adopt a fad like 1-to-1 learning, but that's where their concern for actually coaching, facilitating and teaching Americans ends. Their safety-in-silence stance has allowed provincial interests (money, pseudo-intellectuals) to trump the needs of the generations-after-next, generations that require interconnected, non-stovepipe interdisciplinary studies from the moment they long on to the Internet or set foot in a brick and mortar setting. More's the pity. These legacy educators who dominate policy and curriculum development from kindergarten, college and professional education fear the diffusion of their own power with academic departments, school districts, unions and ivory towers.

Surely there must be some evolutionary/revolutionary minds that remain in the legacy generation that created the educational mayhem that exists in the USA. If they exist, they owe it to new generations to begin the process of opening fronts and building barricades.

One front would include the destruction of the industrial education practices that dominate in America. Assembly-line educational practices that segment into K-8, 9-12, 13-16, 17+ must be eliminated. For example, at the K-12 level, common campus settings that allow older students to interact closely with younger students should be the norm. The notion that "I am a senior and you are just a freshman," needs to go away. This is training for corporation management, not mentoring/teaching. Another front would see the destruction of non-interdisciplinary studies. Humanities and the Sciences, integrated and competently taught, would provide a far more dynamic learning environment for students who government and industry typically malign. A barricade around the Internet and World Wide Web must be built before dominant corporations, politicians, academics and technocrats manage to kill the flow of uncensored information undercuts their power.

Proposed national education standards such as the Common Core Standards supported by President Obama (and Bill Gates) or those represented in the No Child Left Behind Act (President Bush) are nonsensical in a world where both global corporations and the US national security community are, themselves, asking for people who can act and think across time, place and culture. Teaching to a multiple choice test in these times is about as relevant as an IBM punch card. For what purpose is a fact without context and framing?

US Military as Leader in Education: No One has a Better Idea

Standardized testing administered by the American College Board/ETS (SAT) and its rival the ACT must, at some point, be abolished. The genesis of the SAT dates back to World War I and the US Military's need to develop standardized testing to rapidly assess skillsets necessary for Anglo Saxon war fighting abilities: flying, killing, repairing and commanding.

The first official SAT was administered in 1926, according to War Play by Colin Mead (Eamon Dolan, 2013). Eugenicists would use the results of those 1926 tests to cast out Blacks, Asians, Women and assorted White Trash from participating fully in American society. Equally damaging was the near full adoption by America's education leaders--from universities to local school houses--of US military standards of scientific education.

The public and private educators of yesteryear had nothing to offer in place of war and threat based education. The nation was on a mission to conquer all foes. Diverging from that mission was, for many, suicide. Indeed, as Mead reports, such educational and technology transfer from the US military to the population at large was inevitable. World War I, World War II, the Cold War and the War on Terrorism focused all of America's instruments of national power (diplomatic, information, military, economic, financial, law enforcement, intelligence and people) on the goals and objectives necessary to counter or destroy the threat of the day. That included inoculating American minds from the evils of "foreign" thinking. Thus trillions of US dollars were made available to any group or individual who could contribute to the war effort.

And for the most part, over the past 100 years or so the national security based education system has worked out for Americans and, arguably, much of the world. The common core standard running through American educational practice during this time has been threat-centric: a constant threat to America's collective and individual existence, real or imagined, exists and there is a sense of urgency to defeat that threat through education and technology. Even America's instruments of national power are based on threat-centric thinking. In this view the world is trying to take something from every American even though, in reality, Americans have everything the world does not currently have.

The United States remains ascendant today because of, not in spite of, past educational practices that were heavily influenced, if not created, by America's national security enterprise. And there is not a field of study untouched by the US national security machinery. Computer science, telecommunications, anthropology, political science, space science, entertainment, physics, literature and medical practices all owe their beginnings or prosperity to the Department of Defense. This worked for a time.

Bullshit Centric Country: The United States of America

America's threat-centric education paradigm—these days dangerously close to paranoia-- can't be allowed to survive. Recent revelations of the extent of American penetration into the thoughts and dreams of the world—and its own citizens (via the National Security Agency) demonstrate just how out of sync

America is with the world and how close its government mirrors the practices of the once feared Union of Soviet Socialist Republics.

It took a long time but the world, and American citizens, have recently learned just how totalitarian the United State happens to have been and is now. There was a time when corporations and government officials would claim that they could not compete with foreign corporations because of subsidizes provided to them by their own governments. It was all BS of course. Thanks to the NSA--and its collusion with American companies--Americans had access to the bid cost/price, marketing tactics and even a foreign government's support strategy for a particular product.

There is a laundry list of American historical bullshit: Some gems include "we do not torture," "in god we trust," "we have no more important goal than the protection of the American people," "we want to compete in a free and fair market," "we care about the middle class," "our atomic bombs broke the back of the Japanese," "we must protect ourselves from cybersecurity attacks because we are under threat," "we hold our officials accountable," "Google and Verizon value your privacy), "your vote matters", and "we take care of our women and men in uniform."

Secretary of State John Kerry once said that the Internet makes it difficult to govern. Damn straight it should! Without bright, interdisciplinary minds and the Internet and World Wide Web (created by the American defense community and US, British and French scientists/researchers) American government, corporate and academic leaders would have us all believe that they are the "true" champions of freedom. Nothing is further from the truth. Cross disciplinary minds, the Internet and the World Wide Web are the only tools available to counter the false and damaging historical narrative that exists and the one that will surely come in the future if American leaders have their way.

+++++

Sea World Entertainment and Guantanamo Bay: Captivity, Torture and Slow Death

Sea World is under fire after its trainers failed to help a distressed pilot whale stuck on a ledge for at least 25 minutes as the audience watched in horror. The disturbing incident was caught on camera by one attendee who says his view of SeaWorld has been changed forever.--*Huffington Post, 29 July 2013*

I've been on a hunger strike since Feb. 10 and have lost well over 30 pounds. I will not eat until they restore my dignity. I've been detained at Guantanamo for 11 years and three months. I have never been charged with any crime.... I have never received a trial. And there is no end in sight to our imprisonment. Denying ourselves food and risking death every day is the choice we have made. A team from the E.R.F. (Extreme Reaction Force), a squad of eight military police officers in riot gear, burst in. They tied my hands and feet to the bed. They forcibly inserted an IV into my hand. I spent 26 hours in this state, tied to the bed. During this time I was not permitted to go to the toilet. They inserted a catheter, which was painful, degrading and unnecessary. I was not even permitted to pray...no one seriously thinks I am a threat — but still I am here. Years ago the military said I was a "guard" for Osama bin Laden, but this was nonsense, like something out of the American movies I used to watch. They don't even seem to believe it anymore. But they don't seem to care how long I sit here, either. --*New York Times, 13 April 2013*

The documentary Black Fish reminds one that "intelligence" and the human species do not necessarily equate. And it shows just how humanity's bloodthirsty ignorance knows no bounds even in its dealings with a peaceful, incredibly intelligent and social species like the Orcas (Killer Whales). They have not once killed a human being on the high seas, but have done so at Sea World Entertainment, Inc., after the abuse and torture that they have suffered over the years. Some of their human counterparts are captives in Guantanamo Bay.

They are both damaged goods with no options but a slow death.

And their collective fates were, and are, determined at the highest levels of a corporation and its investors (Sea World) and the United States government (POTUS and SECDEF).

That the Killer Whales in captivity at Sea World locations in

Florida are forced to perform for the benefit of tractor-pull audiences is pathetic. Thanks to the American public and private education system for that. Worse still, Black Fish tells the story of how Killer Whales were captured. Rounded up by Sea World's mercenary fishermen the young killer Whales were separated from their mothers, transported by truck to an airport and then flown off to a life in the Sea World pens in Florida. The story and video footage of the carnage and screaming mothers is so gut wrenching that, if one has any empathy and is not a dimwit, the eyes well up with tears and an emotion follows that ignites guilt. It is that painful.

Further into the documentary the audience learns that 70 some "incidents" where trainers were injured have taken place over the decades culminating, as of this writing, in the death of Sea World employee Dawn Brancheau in 2010 (by Tilikum). The US Department of Labor's Occupational Safety and Health Administration (OSHA) filed suit against Sea World claiming that, viewed as a workplace, employees interacting with Killer Whales were in danger of serious injury—including death—because the Killer Whales, ranging in size from 2,000 kilograms to 5,000 kilograms are living, moving heavy machinery interacting with breakable human beings. The death of Brancheau brought the matter to the public's attention. But Black Fish provides much more detail on the "incident" track record dating back to the 1980's. The video footage is astonishing.

The Killer Whales have their own languages and culture—each group is unique. Their life spans are as long as those of human males and females in the United States. Their societies are female dominated. Killer Whale offspring stay with their mothers throughout much of their life spans, according to Black Fish. In two of the most riveting scenes in the documentary Killer Whale children are taken out of the water away from their mothers. The baby screams and cries and the mother does too. More's the pity, the mothers, research showed, sent cries meant for long distance communication in the ocean--an obvious plea for help and sympathy from comrades.

What this does psychologically to the captive female Killer

Whales, certainly tortured by being confined to a large concrete pool and knowing that their child has been kidnapped, can only be imagined. Killer Whales possess a brain that in many respects is far more advanced than those of humans. According to the Center for Whale Research:

"Cetacean brain development is an example of parallel evolution, adapted to the ocean environment. The brains of [Killer Whales] Orca's are roughly four times larger than ours, have a greater surface area relative to brain weight, have enhanced development in different areas, and some of their nerve transmission speeds greatly exceed ours. Naturally enough we humans don't much like the idea that another species might rival us in that which we feel sets us apart from the rest of the animal kingdom: our intelligence..."

US Navy: Killer Whales Make Great Targets

In the book *Sea of Slaughter, author* Farley Mowat indicated that in the 1960's US Navy surface and air units out of Iceland used Killer Whales as live-fire targets. Many Killer Whales were slaughtered along with other whale species. Mowat points out that the US military regularly used large whales for antisubmarine warfare testing. *Sea of Slaughter* also documents the near elimination of Blue Whales and basically the destruction of an entire species more closely related to humans in terms of thought and emotion than the comparably dumb chimpanzee. And when the public got upset with the US military's cavalier attitude to killing and maiming Killer Whales, American military and political leaders could not believe that interest groups would care about preserving a bunch of fish. In that, they echoed the view of the whaling industry whose only concern was short term profit.

The US Navy has continued on with its abuse of aquatic life forms. Attempting to turn dolphins into mine sweepers they have literally brainwashed and abused them. Airlifting them from one combat theater to another, then back again must make the dolphins psychotic. It is madness.

Black Fish informs the audience that Killer Whales in captivity are frequently plucked from different groups with distinct cultures and languages. They are all dumped in a pool together and often do not get along. It is akin to rival gang members being thrown in a jail cell together. Violence ensues. In the Killer Whale's case this means ramming, raking a rival and even taking frustration out on the human handler. Video footage of these troubles is in abundance in Black Fish.

Sea World's biggest investment is in the sperm of the males for breeding purposes. This is why Tilikum who dispensed with Brancheau remains, literally, penned up in a pool at Sea World with an occasional release to perform. Black Fish contains an X-rated scene in which one handler is gently massaging the elongated sexual organ whilst another collects the liquid gold. There are human vampires after all.

Trusted Spin Methodology: The Big Lie

Sea World leaders spin, obfuscate and deny whenever an "incident" threatens the revenue stream. When Sea World Killer Whales are injured (raked) or when their human handlers get killed or taken underwater for long stretches ("play" in the Killer Whale's world), Sea World's leaders blame the underlings. "All their fault, technique was wrong...their mistake" is the refrain, even though the video evidence says otherwise. A good example of this is the notion that Brancheau's pony tail was grabbed by Tilikum to drag her under water. Not correct as the video showed.

It is the same mentality at the lofty heights of the Pentagon: Abu Gharaib was "just the work of a bunch of bad apples." "The United States of America does not torture." "The United States government does collect data on its own people." "We will not kill or torture Edward Snowden." "The 2013 Egypt Coup was not a Coup."

Meanwhile, at the United State's premier Gulag—Guantanamo Bay—the not guilty are held captive with the guilty. They will never walk down a city street again or have a peaceful night's sleep.. They have been tortured repeatedly, some for a decade. Even if released, they are psychologically damned. Dozens (40-45) know this and are on a hunger strike. The *World Medical Association* considers force feeding to be torture. But the Pentagon just doesn't care. Their reply to it all is mechanical, typical, the same sort of formula used by Sea World to justify its treatment of intelligent life: *[We] support the preservation of life by appropriate clinical means, in a humane manner, and in accordance with all applicable law and policy. [The Pentagon] has well-established policies to protect both the detainees and the professional obligations of our medical care providers."*

Getting on into the 21st Century—now the Anthropocene—the human species has staked its claim as one of the most ignorant and immature on the planet. Humans point to massive skyscrapers and sea based oil rigs, supercomputers, genetic engineering, mighty aircraft carriers, stealthy submarines, the Apollo space program and a robot on Mars as crowning achievements for the species. So what!

If the human species kills off most of the life on the planet—disrupting food chains, climate patterns---none of those symbolic "things" will matter at all. The human species knows little about the oceans which cover 70 percent of the planet, yet they are sucking the life out of it by over fishing/whaling, polluting it in the search for energy, deafening its creatures by the use of frequencies painful to their "ears", and dumping garbage and sewage into it. The term "humane" needs to be revised or ditched.

There is much excitement in the scientific community and the popular media about the improvement in the quality of life that genetic and pharmaceutical engineering will bring. Humans can recreate extinct species or those threatened with extinction. But there is no guarantee of that.

Darwin was challenged once with an argument that went something like this: the breeding of animals and plants shows humanity's control over Evolution. Darwin thought about it and said that Evolution will make that judgment over time as the long term consequences can't be known. Humans are not conscious of what may come to pass from their creations, he implied.

But for the moment, one thing is certain, humans are dangerous to themselves and every living creature on the planet

Just ask the Killer Whales.

+++++

Profiting from Food Stamps, Student Loans, Unemployment: Wall Street, US Congress, Obama Cash-in

"Despite being the richest country in the world, poverty remains an important social issue in the United States. All too often poverty in America is used as a political weapon by both political parties to galvanize their voting base. What is lost in the midst of such politicking is the crony connection of corporations that have positioned themselves to profit from poverty. The welfare programs we use to attempt to alleviate poverty actually play directly into the plans of companies that lobby on behalf of legislation lauded as anti-poverty programs. Rather than overcoming poverty, these programs line the pockets of their promoters. Such crony connections must end." Government Accountability Institute

According to the US Census Bureau's Median Value of Debt by Household (2011), the median household debt (both secured and unsecured) for 35-44 year olds was $108,000 (USD); for those 45-54, $86,500; and for 55-64 age group it was $70,000. The data in the Census Bureau report also shows that the less formally educated one is the less debt one has.

The median debt for someone with no high school diploma is $20,000 (with a high school diploma is $42,000), while the median debt for a holder of a graduate or professional degree is $130,705. So while America's educational leaders say that a college degree will likely lead to increased income over the years, they don't mention that secured and unsecured debt increases the "smarter" one becomes.

Debt for You, Profit for Them

Maybe Americans should dump the pursuit of a college degree particularly in the face of rising interest rates for federal student loans and increased tuition and ancillary fees at colleges and universities across the land. High interest rates (the cost of money) on student loans can also serve as a barrier to college entry. Perhaps the "hidden hand of the market" is sending a message of some sort, that the financially sound path is to get an education in the 21st Century trades that combine, say, computers and engines or computer systems and networks. Add a Cisco or Microsoft certification to the tradecraft and a job for life is possible. But buyer beware, earning an Associate's Degree earns you a median debt of $63,000.

Moreover pushing the myth that a college education is a must-have in the USA tends to generate excellent profits for investors, and makes college/university presidents, administrators and senior faculty, quite comfortable. Take the case of Sallie Mae. According to the Huffington Post's September 2013 report *Sallie Mae Profit Boosts College Endowments and Pension Funds As Students Pay More*, "University endowments and teachers' pension funds are among big investors in Sallie Mae, the private lender that has been generating enormous profits thanks to soaring student debt and the climbing cost of education…previously unreported investments [obtained by Huffington Post] mean that education professionals are able to profit twice off the same student: first by hiking the cost of tuition, then through dividends and higher valuations on their holdings in Sallie Mae, the largest student lender and loan servicer in the country, which profits by charging relatively high interest rates on its loans and not refinancing high-rate loans after students graduate and get well-paying jobs. Sallie Mae is a former government-sponsored enterprise that was fully privatized in 2004 and now trades publicly as SLM Corp…

Sallie Mae reported $939 million in net income last year, the highest since 2006. The publicly-traded company, which enjoys a government guarantee on most of its $174 billion in assets, has been profitable in eight of the last 10 years, generating a cumulative $7.3 billion profit. Its shares have risen 54 percent over the past year, outpacing the 19 percent gain in the Standard & Poor's 500 Index, America's benchmark equity gauge…The endowments of Furman University, Harvard University, Mount Holyoke College, and University of Michigan all hold stakes in Sallie Mae through their investments in Highfields Capital Management, a hedge fund that manages more than $11 billion and is the second-biggest Sallie Mae shareholder… Pension funds for teachers and other school employees such as the New York

State Teachers' Retirement System, State Teachers Retirement Board of Ohio, Pennsylvania Public School Employees Retirement System, New Mexico Educational Retirement Board, Teacher Retirement System of Texas and California State Teachers Retirement System (CalSTRS) also own significant chunks of Sallie Mae, as does asset manager TIAA-CREF, which oversees retirement funds for teachers, among others… Federal records show the company spent more than $1.4 million lobbying members of Congress last quarter."

Rockefeller, Obama Nest Eggs Turn Gold

The Government Accountability Institute has an eye-opening study titled *Profits from Poverty: How Food Stamps Benefit Corporations*. Published in September 2012, the report indicates that three corporations dominate the "food stamp market." One of the three, and the largest in the USA, is JP Morgan with 24 state contracts. It is the leading provider of Electronic Benefit Transfers, or EBT's, that channel funds for food to those impoverished Americans that qualify for government assistance. Coming in at the number two slot is Affiliated Computer Services. This firm was acquired by Xerox Corporation in February, 2010. It has a total of 15 state contracts. The third is eFunds Corporation, a subsidiary of Fidelity National Information Services (not connected to Fidelity Investments) and owns 10 state contracts for EBT services and one U.S. territory.

"Originally conceived as a means to prop up sagging crop prices to support American farmers, the Food Stamp Program, now called the Supplemental Nutrition Assistance Program, or SNAP, has exploded into a welfare program that costs tax payers a record $75.67 billion in 2011. Almost everyone has heard this [tired] story, but few realize that only three corporations have cornered the market for providing SNAP services to the needy and destitute. According to JP Morgan, the largest food stamp industry player, the business of food stamps 'is a very important business to JP Morgan. It's an important business in terms of its size and scale…. Right now volumes have gone through the roof in the past couple of years or so. The good news from JP Morgan's perspective is the infrastructure that we built has been able to cope with that increase in volume.' And JP Morgan has good reason to be pleased, since the bank profits from programs designed to help the poor."

SNAP and JP Morgan? SNAP and Xerox? That the poor and needy of America earn profits for JP Morgan and Xerox seems wacky. Welcome to the accelerating Age of Austerity in the USA. Nothing, absolutely nothing must interfere with the free flow of capital in the USA.

More's the pity in this tale of bleeding the middle to lower classes dry is how the political system was used to increase the level of profits for JP Morgan. According to the *Profits of Poverty* report by the *Government Accountability Institute* "[we] uncovered a clear trend of increasing contributions to the Agriculture Committee members of both the [US] House and Senate on the part of JP Morgan…The US Department of Agriculture and its presidential appointees also influence the direction of program policy. This can be seen in the development of broad based categorical eligibility. JP Morgan's donations to political campaigns also show a clear trend. During the 2008 presidential election, Barack Obama received more than twice the contributions of John McCain: $807,000 for Obama compared to McCain's $345,505. After Obama's election, the American Recovery and Reinvestment Act made two important changes to existing SNAP policies. First, it increased SNAP benefits by 13.6 percent. Second, it actively encouraged states to adopt broader rules to increase SNAP caseloads. From 2009 to 2012, 32 states adopted the interpretation. The first change creates a stronger incentive for individuals to enroll for food stamps, and the second change accommodates this increase in enrollment. All of this, working together with an underperforming economy, sets the stage for increasing profits for the companies providing EBT services. The more persons enrolled in the program, the more money the EBT industry makes."

We Need More Poor, Insecure Americans!

Members of the US House and Senate are savvy hustlers, particularly when they are able to rig the system so that corporations can corner markets, reap profits and increase share value. It is a wonderfully devious and perfectly legal system for the rich to get richer and the middling senator or representative to join the ranks of the rich. The *Center for Responsive Politics*, a must visit for anyone wishing to understand how the US political really works, lists the investment portfolios of many in the US Congress. But for an excellent case study in cronyism, we turn back to the *Profits of Poverty* report and the tidy relationship between JP Morgan, Congress and the White House.

"Unfortunately, the crony connections do not stop with congressional lobbying. Several members of Congress and the executive branch have significant investments in JP Morgan stock. President Obama has up to $1 million in a private client asset checking account. In 2010, then White House Chief of Staff William M. Daley also had invested up to $5 million with JP Morgan. In 2007, West Virginia Senator Jay Rockefeller had over $50 million with the bank. Increasing profits for JP Morgan in turn means increasing returns for investors. EBT card systems were guaranteed expansion on December 13, 2010, when President Obama signed the Healthy, Hunger-Free Kids Act. This legislation requires all states to develop and implement the use of EBT cards for the Special Supplemental Nutrition Program for Women, Infants, and Children (WIC) by October 1, 2020. According to the most recent participation data released by the USDA's Food and Nutrition Service, WIC served 8.9 million consumers in FY 2011, which means that EBT card providers are looking at many new customers thanks to the legislation. The expansion of the EBT program did not happen in a vacuum. In fact, JP Morgan was lobbying on issues related to the use of EBT cards in the WIC program during 2009, months before the Healthy-Hunger-Free Kids Act was introduced in the Senate."

Corporations Wage War on Unemployed

American employees are generally viewed by American corporations/businesses as a necessary evil, a burden to the shareholders and profit margins. That view is reflected openly in the US House and Senate, the Executive Branch and even in the US Supreme Court (pro business rulings, *Citizen's United*, etc.). With the Great Recession of 2008 lingering still and with unemployment hovering at 15 percent (unofficial), business owners large and small are not shy about speaking distastefully about the slovenly American worker who wants a living wage, health insurance, some vacation and the security of unemployment benefits when markets leave town.

ADP, the giant payroll and benefits operator in the USA, and around the globe, puts it so, "Your workforce helps you earn money. But it's also costing you a ton of money. So here's the million dollar question: how can you maximize the value of your people and minimize what you spend on managing them?" Stated more bluntly, How can you bleed productivity out of your employee whilst paying him/her as little as possible and reducing benefits?

Equifax is well known to all American employees. Equifax, along with Experian and Trans Union, dominate the credit scoring industry in the USA. Credit scores of the type Equifax provides are not unlike College Board's SAT scores. Both scores are predictors: one for the ability to pay debt with interest, and the other for academic performance at the college/university level. As such, low SAT scores significantly reduce the chances of getting into a long sought after school or even a job (someemployers now require SAT scores). Multiple SAT tests may be required to push up the scores and, of course, the fee based SAT testing means more profit for the College Board. In similar fashion, low credit scores can mean the difference between refinancing a brutal interest-only mortgage loan or not. It may also mean being unable to co-sign for that student loan for the daughter.

Equifax is in the profitable business of fighting on behalf of corporations for unemployment claims. It is also the owner of Talx/Equifax Workforce Solutions which was featured in a New York Times article titled *Contesting Jobless Claims Becomes a Boom Industry*. Equifax apparently engaged in underhanded practices aimed at individuals claiming unemployment benefits. Hearings are typically conducted at the state level to determine the legitimacy of claims but employers do not normally have the staff available to attend and protest them all. Enter Equifax: its website states that for one company it serviced "in 2009, the increase in the number of hearings attended resulted in $342,676 in liability avoided. For 2010, this amount was $663,913."

The street offers the only escape. Otherwise: Workers of the World! Capitulate!

+++++

About the Author

John Stanton lives in the Washington, DC Metropolitan region. He has written hundreds of articles on national security and political matters. He taught a course on national security for nine years at a private school. His commentary has been carried by radio, television and the world wide web. John's works are cited in scores of publications relating to national security issues. Visit academia.edu for more information.

www.ingramcontent.com/pod-product-compliance
Lightning Source LLC
Chambersburg PA
CBHW071354310526
45790CB00017B/387